D1456244

Ballroom Dancing

Ballroom Dancing

THE ROMANCE, RHYTHM AND STYLE

JOHN LAWRENCE REYNOLDS

Principal Photography by Xavier Nuez

and John Lawrence Reynolds

LAUREL
GLEN

For Jacob Wolfenden,
whose toes already twinkle

This edition published in 1998 in the United States by
Laurel Glen Publishing
5880 Oberlin Drive, Suite 400
San Diego, CA 92121-9653
1-800-284-3580

Library of Congress Cataloging in Publication Data

Reynolds, John (John Lawrence)
    Ballroom dancing: the romance, rhythm and style / John Lawrence Reynolds
        p.   cm.
        Includes index.
        ISBN 1-57145-621-X

1. Ballroom dancing. 2. Dance-Sociological aspects. I. Title.

GV1751.R46   1998   98-17096
                            CIP

First published in Canada in 1998 by Key Porter Books Limited

Printed and bound in China

98 99 00 01 02   5 4 3 2 1

The photographs on pages 8–9, 26–27, 33, 35–37, 42, 51, 70–71, 76–77, 84–85, 92–93, 100–101, 110–111, 127, 158–159, 175, 178, 183, and 184 are by Xavier Nuez; those on pages 60–61 are by Jaro Steigler; and those on pages 113 and 120 are by David Mark. The remainder are by the author.

Contents

Acknowledgments

EVERYONE I ENCOUNTERED in the competitive dance world was supportive and wonderfully cordial during the preparation of this book. I am grateful to them all for their kind assistance and patient guidance. Several, however, deserve individual recognition.

Robert Tang and Beverley Cayton-Tang were superbly helpful and encouraging, and the best qualities of this book are a direct result of their contribution. In addition to being championship dancers, they are warm and generous people.

Ann Harding and Wendy Johnson were equally gracious in explaining the world of competitive dance and judging procedures. Marcus and Karen Hilton, along with Bob Powers and Julia Gorchakova, provided valuable insight into the dancing life from their perspective and patiently endured my selfish interruptions during competitions.

I am indebted to Edna and Derek Cayton for their Blackpool hospitality; Akiko Stewart-Morris and her husband Malcolm for their good-humored encouragement; David Mark, Mi Ki and Susan Kan, and Ron Self for their photographic assistance; Juliet McMains for her academic papers and commentary; plus Lee Wakefield, Joy and Colin Fielding, Sandi Brittain, Sara Wolstenholme, Tom Murdock, Judy Hattin, Gillian MacKenzie, and Bev and Jaro Steigler for all their assistance.

Thanks as well to Susan Renouf, Michael Mouland and Jean Lightfoot Peters at Key Porter Publishing for their professional expertise and personal empathy.

Finally, thanks to the two most important people in any writer's life: my agent, Jan Whitford, who makes it all possible; and my wife, Judy, who makes it all worthwhile.

J.L.R.

CHAPTER ONE

Private Emotions in a Public Space

I would like to sit under a tree,
drink wine, and watch people dance.
—Adlai Stevenson

WE ALL DANCE.

We tap our toes to insistent rhythms and drum our fingers on the steering wheel of our car without a thought, responding to something within ourselves that is both primeval and elegant. Primeval because the roots were generated by the soothing presence of our mother's heartbeat in the womb and at the breast; elegant because in no other endeavor does the human body move with the grace of an inspired dance performed by gifted artists.

We all dance, whether as a rite of courtship or a manifestation inspired by a celebration, or even a less formal occasion.

Dancing is a lifelong celebration for most. The sight of a young child dancing in the presence of encouraging adults is pure delight, and the vision of a couple devoted to each other throughout their long lives, dancing among members of their family to songs heard only within their hearts and their memories, is inspiring, almost spiritual.

Social dancing is performed for personal pleasure. Ballroom dancing, especially at the higher competitive levels, is performed as much for the pleasure of those who watch as for those who participate. The two are linked, but the linkage extends across a gulf as vast as the distance between a community tennis club and Wimbledon.

In recent years, ballroom dancing has been expanding steadily, almost subversively, until it stands poised for an explosion of coverage by mass media in North America and possible recognition as a competitive Olympic event. No one who has witnessed competitive dancing at the highest level can avoid the impression that these are both artists and athletes. We are drawn to ballroom dancing, performed at the zenith of ardor and skill, because the participants express themselves in a manner beyond our ability and even, to some degree, beyond our comprehension. They perform figures and swirls that move our souls, while we cannot motivate our bodies in the same graceful and abandoned manner.

Yet we are dancers all, if only in the theaters of our minds.

MEN AND WOMEN EXPRESSED THEMSELVES by dancing long before the use of written language, or perhaps any language at all. The act of dancing conveys essential elements of our lives as social animals, especially those desires and emotions that defy expression in other ways.

Among ancient peoples, the act of dancing prepared warriors for battle, sought appeasement from powerful gods and spirits, or simply enabled the participants to share feelings of joy and delight. By the rise of modern Euroethnic society, these emotions and expressions had been distilled into ballet, which we accept as the elevation of dance to its ultimate level. But ballet, for all its majestic refinement, remains an abstraction or representation of dancing's basic roots. Ballet represents a ritualistic idiom performed in a fantasy world circumscribed by a theatrical stage. We admire the routines of ballet in much the same way as we absorb the production of a Shakespearean historical play: the content is both profound and familiar, and we find ourselves judging not so much the interpretation of the performers as their vitality, their technical skill, and their journey through a landscape we all know but can never inhabit.

But we can all venture onto the dance floor, and when we do, in our various, sometimes awkward ways, we sample the appeal of dance firsthand. On these social occasions, skill counts less than enthusiasm. It is not necessary at times like these to dance well, only to participate. What is a wedding celebration, after all, without dancing?

Ballroom dancing acknowledges this communal spirit, even at its highest competitive level. Every ballroom dance event includes frequent breaks for "general dancing." For a time, the intense rivalry of the competing teams is set aside as partners, coaches, judges, and members of the audience step onto the floor, immersing themselves in the simple joy of dancing to the rhythm of music whose message is not rebellion, but romance.

ROMANCE REMAINS THE ESSENTIAL core of dance, whatever the origins of the individual steps. It represents the heart of competitive ballroom dancing, or "DanceSport" as many adherents prefer, and may account for its expanding popularity. Amid the youth-oriented, in-your-face rebellion of gangsta rap, hip-hop rhythms, and bloodless electronic melodies, the music of ballroom dancing represents a refuge for romance. Successful DanceSport competitors draw upon a vast range of personal qualities, and perhaps the most universal yet elusive is a strong romantic character. With it, they achieve ultimate heights of expression, their bodies unconsciously celebrating the passion in their hearts; without it, they become programmed automatons, precise in their moves yet leaving us strangely indifferent.

The romantic quotient, in fact, may be the only common element among contemporary ballroom dancers at the competitive level. From that point, dancing divides and subdivides into styles and schools.

The first division is easy and distinct: couples specialize in either Standard or Latin styles. In the United States, this breaks down further into American Smooth, a derivative of Standard; and American Rhythm, with modified Latin dances. Superbly

gifted and ambitious couples compete in both, which means they must excel at ten different dance steps.

Standard and American Smooth dances include those traditionally associated with ballrooms: waltz (both "slow" and Viennese), fox-trot, tango, and quick-step. (American Smooth drops the quick-step.) Most can be traced back to royal courts and elegant salons, with the exception of the tango—but the tango is always an exception.

In competitive ballroom performances for these dances, male partners move as regally as one can while wearing a set of tails, vest, bow tie, and stiff plastic collar. The demeanor of the men reflects their costume. While male dancers may express various degrees of pleasure during the dance performance—confident joy in the quick-step and fox-trot, subdued delight in the waltz, remote satisfaction during the tango—their carriage is consistently upright and steadfast. This stoicism suggests a form of military discipline reminiscent of a time when cavalry officers were drawn from men of good breeding, which meant they were as well-versed in social graces as in battle.

Visualize male dancers in eighteenth-century military dress, all fringed epaulets and polished sabers instead of black tuxedos, and the image crystallizes. In fact, military dress itself is responsible for the traditional stance of Standard dancers; the male's left hip meets the female's right hip, thus keeping his right hip open for access to his sword—and, of course, for the comfort of his female partner.

Male Standard and American Smooth dancers must conform with other males in near-identical ebony tail suits, but their female partners glow with stunning individuality. Here, all is presentation. The women wear exquisitely designed gowns cut to emphasize and exaggerate each motion of their body even while concealing it among folds and fringes. They frame their faces amid sparkling jewels, embellish their features with the heavy application of stage cosmetics, and slide their feet into narrow-heeled, suede-soled pumps.

The facial expressions of women dancers contrast sharply with the sterner expressions of their partners. During the waltz

Competitive ballroom dancing demands much of each partner: poise, glamour, athletic prowess, and, during Standard dances, a certain stoicism from the men.

and quick-step, women are expected to portray unbridled jubilation that threatens to explode into euphoria as they glide around the floor, secure within their partners' embrace. They smile with pure delight, frequently offering themselves to their partners with an "oversway," achieved by throwing back their head and shoulders, appearing to support their weight entirely in the man's arms while gazing, one presumes, upward to heaven. For the woman, all must be gaiety and pleasure, all must appear spontaneous and effortless even while ankles scream in protest, calves knot into cramps, and shoes pinch the toes like a vise.

On the surface, this is romance in the fantastic literary tradition. The man leads, and the woman dutifully follows. The man conquers, the woman surrenders. The man must always be taller and dominant, the woman smaller and submissive.

These apparent male/dominant, female/submissive roles make some feminists uncomfortable. They point out, for example, that the vocabulary of dancing is defined from the perspective of the male leader. When a couple is described or directed as moving forward in a progressive dance—that is, one in which the couple moves across or around the floor—it is understood that the male is moving forward and the female is moving backward. Descriptions of dance figures, such as a "*chasse* to the left," signify that the man is moving to his left and the woman to her right. Another common step, a "forward lock," means the man is moving forward while the woman (presumably) moves backward.

More strident critics even decry the fact that competing couples are invariably identified by numbers pinned to the *man's* back. Given the almost universal bare-backed design of contemporary women's gowns, one wonders where and how the numbers might otherwise be applied, but feminists draw clear parallels between competitive dance couples being identified by the male's number and married couples assuming the man's surname.

In reality, the male/female leader/follower roles are less a reflection of formal tradition than a practical matter on the dance

In the midst of swirls and turns, women ignore the discomfort of binding gowns and high-heeled shoes to express unbridled jubilation.

The American Smooth style emphasizes individual expression, encouraging partners to break into improvised movements.

floor. Truly successful competitive dancing couples perform as a single entity, united in equal skill and status, and the successful performance of a female partner may place far greater demands on her than on the male dancer. As a popular feminist slogan put it: "Ginger did everything Fred did, except she did it backwards while wearing high heels."

"STANDARD" DANCES ARE FREQUENTLY referred to as International style to distinguish them from American style—in this case, American Smooth. The roots of American Smooth reach back to the rise of major U.S. studio chains such as Arthur Murray and Fred Astaire following World War II. These studios, seeking to replicate the flamboyance practiced by Astaire in his popular movies, dropped the quick-step from the repertoire and abandoned the tradition of dancers always maintaining a closed position for every step. In closed position, the partners face each other throughout the dance, never "breaking" from their loose embrace. American Smooth encourages frequent breaks from the closed position, permitting the partners to improvise and dance without any physical contact between them—a common feature of Latin dances.

American Smooth influenced more than dancing styles. It led to functional and design differences in women's ball gowns as well. International Standard dances, performed exclusively in closed position, conceal the front of a woman's gown from others and thus reduce its visual importance. To add drama to their gowns, International dancers seek dresses festooned with feather boas, floats, or drapes around the arms and shoulders, and other accoutrements to draw attention from judges and spectators.

Such accessories are a hindrance to American Smooth performers. Floats and drapes that add grace and drama when the arms are held at shoulder level become a hindrance when the arms are lowered, or when the partners break and circle each other. As a result, American Smooth gowns tend toward more spectacular color and style, especially around the bodice. In addition, the skirts are split often to hip level to reveal the woman's legs as she spins.

All of this makes the American Smooth style especially attractive to television coverage. The TV camera loves the motion and color of a swirling taffeta or chiffon gown, not to mention the thrill of a dancer's legs suddenly, briefly exposed. Not surprisingly, extensive television coverage of competitive dance events in North America is expected to stimulate the growth of American Smooth at the expense of International Standard dances.

LATIN DANCERS HAVE NO NEED for different costumes when performing either International Latin or American Rhythm style. Skimpy dresses and hip-hugging trousers serve equally well for both International Latin (cha-cha, samba, rumba, paso doble, and jive) and American Rhythm (cha-cha, samba, rumba, and jive or swing—with bolero, mambo and merengue added from time to time).

If Standard dances echo the formalities and rituals of royal courts and upper-class salons, Latin and American Rhythm dances reflect life in the barrios of Havana, the streets of Rio, the bullfight arenas of Granada, and the nightclubs of Harlem.

In Latin dances, courtship remains the language, but the message is often pure lust. First-time spectators at professional-level Latin competitions are often stunned by the unbridled energy, athletic prowess, and open eroticism of the dancers. Beginning in the hips and pelvis, the nonstop motion bursts like an electrical force down to the legs and feet and up through the chest, shoulders, eyes, and mouth, flashing from the fingertips like lightning.

The costumes of Latin dancers underscore the passion. Men choose blousy shirts, unbuttoned to display rippling pectorals, and trousers that flatten the stomach while sculpting the buttocks. Women select costumes that emphasize both the sensuality of the dance steps and the superb physique of their bodies, sometimes carrying it to almost outrageous lengths. The effect is intentionally shocking and disarming.

It is easy—but erroneous—to assume that all Latin/Rhythm dances are mere variations on musically energized fertility rites. In reality, Latin dances are as subtle in their message and as

Less is more when it comes to
Latin costumes for female dancers,
drawing attention to the sensuality
of the movements as well as to the
dancers' taut and muscular
physiques.

deliberate in their competitive mandates as the more sedate Standard dances.

WHENEVER THE FUTURE development of ballroom dancing is discussed, it is usually measured against the recent evolution of figure skating. From a closed-culture, single-season pastime of the 1930s and 1940s, figure skating has burst into a new, virtually year-round television spectacle. This development established a target for DanceSport advocates and detractors alike. No one doubts skating's identity as both a popular media attraction and a serious competitive activity—a situation that many fans of competitive dancing would like to see emulated on the ballroom floor. Nor does anyone question figure skating's qualifications as a major Olympic event.

But is *dancing* truly a sport? Its advocates make a very convincing case.

Sport suggests athleticism, and the athletic demands placed on dancers at the competitive level are astonishing. Their physical condition and training regimen compares with those of Olympic participants in any track and field event you choose to name.

Consider the frenetic activity of competitive Latin dancing. Five dances comprise the Latin competition, and the final is always jive or swing, the most arduous of all. Competitive jive dancing has more in common with gymnastics than with ballet—the dancers are tossed, spun, twirled, and somersaulted to insistent rock-and-roll rhythms. Placing jive last in the five Latin dance steps is a near-sadistic test of the dancers' stamina. Competitors must not reveal any lagging of energy or spirit in their performance, even after exhausting presentations of the cha-cha, mambo, rumba, and paso doble.

Less apparent are the physical demands placed on participants in International Standard or American Smooth dance events. We may admire the elegance of the waltz and the precise formality of the tango, but how strenuous are these graceful steps, and how important are the physical condition and athleticism of the dancers?

With DanceSport drawing more television attention, the medium is certain to alter both public appreciation and competition structure.

Substantially more than one might expect. One German study noted that each dancer performing a three-minute quickstep exerts as much energy as a competitor in an 800-meter run. Of course, the runner is not required to wear suede-bottomed shoes (with three-inch heels for the females) and stiff-collared tuxedos or layered gowns. Nor is the runner asked to compete in four other consecutive events, all within the space of twelve minutes or less.

WILL THE GROWTH OF COMPETITIVE DANCING in North America rival the success of professional figure skating? The decision may lie with television.

In athletics and entertainment, some events are better suited for television coverage than others. Football and basketball are ideal TV subjects, awash with brilliant color and near-constant motion. Baseball and fencing are less appropriate sports, although baseball survives in seriously modified form.

Curiously, if one were asked to name all the ideal qualities for a competitive event on television, the reply likely would incorporate every aspect of DanceSport: vibrant color, constant motion, intense competition, male/female partners, overt sensuality, and stimulating music, all performed within the confines of a controlled environment.

Similar qualities propelled figure skating to remarkable levels of popularity, thanks to sponsored network television programming. Barely a generation ago, figure skating was a once-a-year event on prime-time TV. Today, rarely does a week pass without coverage of some skating competition, usually a heavily endorsed event whose primary function is to provide a full hour's exposure of the sponsor's name painted at center ice.

For various reasons, ballroom dancing has failed to achieve *any* level of recognition on North American television beyond the annual Ohio Star Ball on PBS and periodic coverage by local cable stations. The situation is dramatically different in other parts of the world.

In Germany, weekly competitive ballroom dancing coverage

draws more than four million television viewers per show, ranking it second only to soccer in audience size. While entire households of German, French, and Italian fans of DanceSport sit absorbed in front of their Telefunken TV sets, almost a million Britons are practicing at one of eight thousand ballroom dance studios in the United Kingdom—or catching their country's own coverage of ballroom dancing on the BBC, on a long-running show titled "Come Dancing." When the BBC announced the cancellation of "Come Dancing" in 1996, viewer protests erupted with such vehemence that the show was quickly restored to the network's schedule.

In Japan, the careers of the country's top competitive dance couples are followed by dance enthusiasts as closely as any movie star's. One source estimates that forty thousand Japanese amateurs and twelve thousand Japanese professionals engage in competitive dancing, a substantial number of them traveling to far corners of the globe to participate in DanceSport events.

In cities, towns, and villages throughout Australia, Eastern Europe, Southeast Asia, and South America, the music of Cole Porter, George Gershwin, Jerome Kern, and Billy Joel drifts through open windows of dance studios. On balmy evenings, the sound of suede-soled shoes sliding across a waxed floor can be heard above the quiet incantations of dance instructors to their students: "...and *turn* and *turn* and *step* and ... *Yes*, you've got it!"

Why has competitive ballroom dancing, or DanceSport, failed to achieve similar recognition in North America? Does the problem spring from one of those strange social chasms that separate cultures as effectively as any ocean? Not necessarily.

DanceSport in North America is practiced, pursued, and profited from by an impressive number of devotees, even if network television denies its existence by refusing to cover its major events. More than three hundred closed or open ballroom dancing competitions are held annually in North America, attracting more than thirty thousand registered dancers. U.S. cities such as Columbus, Ohio, and Savannah, Georgia, host major dance

Rapport between dancers is essential, whether driven by romantic attraction to each other or simply by a shared passion for the dance.

festivals each year, and their several hundred competitors arrive from countries all over the world.

What, then, is the barrier to wider recognition? Why can't DanceSport "break out"? Television is obviously the key. And North American television is driven by money as surely as electricity powers the TV studio's lights and cameras.

The emergence of figure skating as a virtual year-round attraction was nurtured by substantial contributions from television programming sponsors. Figure skating meets all the demands of mass-market sponsors: it's competitive, glamorous, fast-moving, tension-filled, and, for the most part, easy for novice viewers to follow and understand.

As a result, Olympic skating champions and near-champions, whose career length had previously been measured within the span of a single Olympiad, now enjoy a profession that rewards them with long-term fame and fortune. Ten years after her Olympic gold medal performance in Calgary, Katarina Witt remains a popular, crowd-building competitor at professional figure skating events around the globe.

Can DanceSport achieve equal status in terms of widespread recognition and support, and generate substantial purses and endorsement fees for its professional competitors? And even if it can, should it? The question spawns vehement arguments, with one camp declaring that the sport and its participants deserve rewards of fame and fortune, the other deriding the danger of "selling out" to sponsors and media moguls.

Another concern addresses the question of tradition. Competitive ballroom events, even at the highest levels, are surprisingly casual, almost folksy productions. Spectators sit at floor level, and if sight lines in ballrooms are less than ideal, proximity and lighting make up for the problems of poor seating arrangements. The biggest names in DanceSport may be seated next to you in the audience or sweeping by you on the dance floor during "general dancing." General dancing is one of the charming carryovers from the time when all dancing was social. Today, even the most exclusive and prestigious dance competitions include periods in which everyone present is invited onto the floor to participate in a waltz or fox-trot, whatever their level of skill and finesse.

Television coverage, in the aggressive U.S. network style, will change all that. In some venues it already has.

The presence of a full-coverage network television crew in any environment is less like a harmless "fly on the wall" and more like a six-hundred-pound gorilla. At competitive dancing events, television technicians and their equipment occupy the best viewing locations. The lighting grows more intense and dramatic, boom-mounted remote-controlled cameras hover near the dancers' shoulders like curious electronic aliens, and the audience reactions are virtually scripted by the show's directors, alternately encouraged and restricted. "Please do not mill around and gossip," spectators may be warned at one point, then "Let's applaud loudly and more vigorously!" they're instructed at another. The social aspects of dancing quickly dissolve into the demands of show business.

BALLROOM DANCING APPEALS to spectators because of its unique combination of fixed and improvised qualities. The fixed qualities are dictated by the music and syllabus for the dance; the improvised aspects are the product of the couples' talents, teamwork, ingenuity, and intuition.

When the music begins, the dance partners engage in something between an athletic performance and an intimate conversation. Custom and ritual direct the male to assume the lead and the female to respond. But among gifted dancing couples, inflexible choreography is unheard of. Even during rigid and rehearsed dance steps, an improvised or intuitive gesture by one partner may produce an impulsive reaction from the other and launch a new, unanticipated sequence of motions and maneuvers to be explored.

DanceSport demands equal participation by both partners and both hemispheres of the brain. The logical, linear side adheres to the rhythm, tempo, and established steps of the dance being performed—the quick three-beats-to-the-bar of the Viennese waltz, the sedate rise-and-fall motions of the Standard or Smooth waltz, the joyful bouncing cousin-of-the-polka quick-step, the liquid motions of the fox-trot, and the ritualized hormonal zest of the tango. These represent the established perimeters, the immutable foundation of each step.

True dancing genius springs from each partner's other brain hemisphere, the one in charge of intuition and expression. This is the uniquely human aspect of the dance, largely unscripted and unpredictable, like human nature itself. Sudden improvisation occurs even among the most rehearsed and experienced dancing partners, who practice over and over again the facial demeanors likely to attract high marks from judges: exhilarating smiles for waltzes and fox-trots, impassivity in the tango, fervent emotions in most Latin steps. But during the intense moments of competition, skilled dancers may surprise each other with a sudden graceful gesture or a thrilling new variation.

In this sense, DanceSport is akin to the best of sophisticated improvisational jazz, in which neither the listener nor the performer knows how the next musical phrase will sound. Then, once heard, the spontaneous melody seems immediately logical and inevitable.

UNTOLD HOURS OF PRACTICE in mirrored dance halls and odoriferous school gymnasiums finally lead to the moment when the man fastens a number to his back, the woman makes a last inspection of her mascara and hemline, and together they move to the edge of the ballroom floor. They may nervously cling to each other's hand or stand apart, surveying the competition. They may be married or engaged to each other, married or engaged to other partners, once married to each other and now connected only by the dance.

But when the music begins, it matters not. They assume their positions, touching at the hip for Smooth or Standard dances, posturing in planned passion for the first of the Latin steps, before their bodies begin responding to something more than the music.

They are about to assume identities they lacked just a few moments ago. As the music plays, he becomes the sophisticated yet approachable man about town and she is the girl next door, innocently beguiling or provocatively enticing. They are Fred and Ginger, and their motions over the next several minutes, through five contrasting rhythms and steps, enchant those who watch from the gallery and, they hope, those who judge their proficiency from the edge of the parquet floor.

At its peak their performance evolves into something only the most fortunate of us experience: a union of two individuals, demonstrating skill and expressing personal emotions across a private space for public consumption.

CHAPTER TWO

Footsteps on the Floor

ANYONE CAN RISE FROM THEIR table at a wedding or a country club function, take a partner's hand, and walk confidently onto the dance floor. Through multiple choruses of one tune after another, they may dance with wildly varying degrees of style, talent, and enthusiasm.

Those who swirl under the lights and over the dance floor may be experts or novices. But at whatever level, dancing is becoming an increasingly popular pastime.

Exciting and enjoyable it may be, but ballroom dancing it is not.

Couples whose prowess has not altered much since high school dances in the gymnasium may consider ballroom dancing an exotic endeavor, practiced for the most part either by athletic exhibitionists or by lonely singles enticed to dance studios by promises of social fulfillment.

Neither extreme is entirely true, nor is the gulf between weekend social dancers and ballroom aficionados nearly as wide or as deep as may appear at first glance. True, successful DanceSport competitors are gifted and dedicated athletes. But this needn't discourage anyone who has watched from the sidelines of a dance floor and wished, in some small corner of their souls, they could perform the basic steps of a samba or fox-trot.

The study of any art form, from music and dancing through literature and painting, should be pursued first for its own sake, for the private and individual pleasure it brings, and for the way it shapes character and personality.

Ballroom dancing is like that. If we stand on the sidelines and simply wish, nothing will change. If we choose to participate without training and practice, growing merely frustrated, nothing will be learned. But if we move past the twin barriers of intimidation and frustration, we may discover new vistas, new pleasures, and new aspects of ourselves and others.

THE CONCEPT OF THE SELF-TAUGHT genius is almost inevitably a myth. We all require mentors and tutors to identify our strengths and weaknesses, and to convey proven ideas of technique and concept.

But whereas few people hesitate to seek lessons in contract bridge or haute cuisine if those pursuits occupy their interest, many shrink from the idea of ballroom dancing lessons. Perhaps they are deterred by the fear of high-pressure sales techniques practiced by some unscrupulous studios, or by the notion that dance studios are a last refuge for lonely people seeking companionship.

Things are changing, thank goodness. The United States Ballroom Dance Association (USBDA) estimates that the number of active dancers under thirty years of age more than doubled between 1990 and 1997. Not long ago, the average age of students at Arthur Murray studios was sixty-five, and 80 percent of them were single. In 1997, the Arthur Murray organization reported this average had dropped to thirty-five years of age, and 60 percent were couples. In 1987, only 200 couples in the United States were professional ballroom dancers. Ten years later the number of professional couples had exploded to 1,600, with more than 12,000 registered amateur competitors.

On a global basis, the growth of dancing is even more impressive. In mid-1997 the Paris-based International DanceSport Federation (IDSF) estimated that 9 million people

Dance is booming around the world, and extensive TV coupled with Olympic recognition are certain to lift its appeal for all ages.

worldwide were registered for DanceSport events; of these, 230,000 couples were licensed as teachers, coaches, adjudicators, and in other key roles.

This may be merely the effect of aging baby boomers seeking physical activity and social opportunities. But it is quite likely more than that. The growth of ballroom dancing may well be anchored in something more basic than exercise and companionship.

Interest in ballroom dancing is undoubtedly inspired by a

At every level, dancing remains a kinetic form of body language, structured according to rhythm and melody.

revived feeling, perhaps even a *yearning*, for beauty, harmony, and rhythm in our lives. There was a time, after all, when these three elements of a joyful life were sought—and found—in many aspects of popular entertainment. Broadway musicals, elaborate film productions, and challenging theatrical presentations once employed them routinely. Popular composers of the 1930s such as Jerome Kern, George Gershwin, Cole Porter, and Richard Rodgers all infused their work with a respect for beauty, harmony, and rhythm. Except for periodic double entendres by Porter to gently nudge the vestiges of Victorian taste, none of their work was the least bit rebellious.

Sixty years later rebellion has become the norm, fueled by the power of a youth-oriented entertainment industry. Rebellion has little use for languid rhythms, sentimental lyrics, or complex haunting chords. Rebellion demands power and spectacle, and both Broadway and Hollywood respond with elaborate technical extravaganzas. Entire cities explode on movie screens and chandeliers shatter onstage, while budgets and profits balloon to incomprehensible proportions.

Contrast these contemporary theatrics and movie magic with the simple appeal of two people lost in romance.

Ballroom dancing is all about romance. It is also about music, art, and high fashion, plus discipline, grace, exercise, and some inner yearnings that most dancers are unable to articulate because, they feel, it has all been said in the doing.

"Why do you love to dance?" one asks, and the response is frequently: "Watch me on the floor—my feet, my body, my hands, and especially my face. Watch my eyes. *Watch my smile!*"

We are all familiar with body language as a silent expression of unarticulated emotions. It takes no leap of faith to view dancing as a kinetic form of body language, unique in its ability to communicate with our partners, others on the dance floor, and those watching from the sidelines.

This is the essence of dancing, not where you place your feet or how you grasp your partner. Dancing remains a superb personal expression, framed within the confines of the floor and structured by the rhythm and melody of the music.

On the competitive dance floor, attitude is everything—intense and assured, yet relaxed and intuitive.

Attitude is especially heightened in Latin dances. This is no place for the timid, especially for male dancers, whose manner must be confident to the point of domination.

Many dance teachers, understanding this essence, advise their students to "begin from the inside." By this they mean their students should not attempt to imitate all the moves of other dancers, even while executing the same basic steps. Conscious imitation eliminates the inner joy of spontaneity, producing stiffness and tension. Dancing is not about stiffness and tension; it is about suppleness and relaxation.

Beginning from the inside permits all the honesty of one's

body language to express itself. For many beginners, the sole emotion to be expressed is uncertainty and nervousness, but it matters not.

Beginning from the inside means being true to oneself. When dancing, every emotion is expressed through muscle action, the transformation of feelings into body movement. Without this transformation, a perfectly executed dance will be less than inspired for either the performer or the audience.

Stanislavsky revolutionized the art of acting by stating that emotion follows one of two paths: from the body to the soul, and from the soul to the body. The same paths are followed when dancing. With the former, you are instructed to "Get up and dance," and in response you trudge onto the floor, methodically commanding your feet to move in time to the music and your body to respond in kind. In the latter, rhythm and harmony inspire you to rise and acknowledge the effects of the music on your soul, tapping and releasing inner emotions.

Ideally, dancing expresses beauty of both body and soul in a magic balance of lyricism and physics. No other activity quite matches dancing in this manner. Nor is any other activity as available, in one degree or another, to virtually everyone who is physically able to pursue it.

IN SERIOUS DANCE COMPETITION, attitude is key. The competitive ballroom dance floor is no place for the hesitant— not beyond the first dance heat, at least. Dancing must be performed with an assuredness and confidence that identifies the couple as masters of their entire domain, a domain defined by the limits of the dance floor and enclosed in glamour, music, and romance.

In competitive dancing, each step must appear to be made with total confidence. Within the shelter of this special aura the couple can move with all the sharply focused intent of a single mind, two bodies expressing the selfsame emotion, all circumscribed within melody and rhythm.

The music and dance steps define the necessary expression and attitude. During waltzes and the quick-step, the couple is

expected to exude sheer heaven-sent bliss in each other's arms. When performing in American Smooth competitions, the man and woman break from the closed position as though inspired by a sudden explosion of joy. Their parallel steps and responsive figures represent a kinetic interpretation of their relationship, so close and abiding that they think and move like a single personality.

The fox-trot may also be performed with an expression of happiness based on the couple's relationship and on their total confidence in each other's intent and ability, although many dancers turn down the bliss control a little here, seeking a deeper resonance of love and romance.

All joy is abandoned in the tango, however. Here the couple's eyes never dare to meet, and their expressions are fixed and immutable, severe and merely tolerant. This is a serious pastime, practiced by those with little to gain and nothing to lose—especially innocence and trust.

It is all a game, of course, but a game as deeply rooted in the traditions and expression of the dance as the costumes they wear and the figures they execute. Perform the quick-step with a severe expression, and everyone will suspect you are suffering from indigestion. Glide across the floor during the Argentine or Standard tango with your head tossed and a smile of delirious delight, and you identify yourself as someone with no respect for the dance and all that it represents.

Performing Latin dances demands an even wider range of expressed emotions, and the most successful Latin dancers excel at their response to each other—although the primary objects of their expressions are the judges and audience. Dancing the cha-cha demands a coy, innocent sexuality, almost adolescent in its presentation and joyous in its effect. The flow is reversed in the samba, where the dance seems to begin with joy and leads to sexual awakening. The rumba is serious in its intent, a dance of passion and seduction. In at least its defiant attitude, the paso doble is the equivalent of the tango, with much posturing and dramatic effects and little sense of frivolity. Finally, jive and swing are pure joy. In these steps, the dancers

The sheer pleasure of the dance, and the joy of mastering new steps, never fades.

burst with exuberance at their youth, their skill, their beauty, their energy, and their spontaneous response to the power and drive of the music.

WHEN IS IT TOO LATE to learn dancing?

Probably never, as long as the student accepts some basic concepts and banishes a few destructive beliefs.

One approach is to see dance as a controlled progression across the dance floor. This does not suggest that dancing is merely walking to music. "Controlled progression" involves using different parts of the feet according to the kind of progress being made—straight, turning, spinning, rising, or lowering. When advancing across the floor, the body remains positioned while a moving leg provides direction and a stationary leg provides power. Picture these actions in your mind, and some of the mystery of dancing begins to vanish.

But dancing is not exclusively footwork, just as conversation is not exclusively words. Beginning dancers concentrate on the movement of their feet because, without understanding this action, no progress can be made. When the footwork becomes so natural that it no longer occupies the center of the dancer's consciousness, grace and expression begin to assume prominence.

Consider a dancer's arms. Employed in the same way that tightrope walkers use their arms when carrying a balance pole, the arms and the balance pole become an extension of the body. The body controls the arms, not vice-versa. Dancers who precisely follow the exact steps of a dance at the exact tempo create an impression of awkwardness and deficiency when their arms attempt to direct their body.

In some dances, the arms fulfill critical functions. During the paso doble, the arms accentuate certain passages in the music, helping to interpret the specialized role of each partner. When dancing the waltz, fox-trot, or other Standard dances in the closed position—partners facing each other with all four hands in contact—the arms determine the shoulder lines.

All of this is directed toward fluidity, a sense of coordinated

Every sophisticated city once boasted a retinue of grand ballrooms for public dancing. Now only a handful survive, and few approach the grandeur of Blackpool's famed Winter Gardens.

and constant movement in direct response to the rhythm of the music. At a certain level, both in social and competitive dancing, the partners are so attuned to each other and to their graceful motions that they respond unconsciously with movements that create and even emphasize fluidity. Watch a gifted (and usually well-practiced) couple dance and you soon recognize subtleties of motion that not even the dancers are aware of. A woman in a long-skirted ball gown, for example, may be spun by her partner, the action raising the hem of the gown up and out. As she spins the man rises on his toes, mimicking the gown's action. When she ceases spinning the hem descends, and as it does the man descends to his heels and perhaps bends his knees a little, creating a sense of constant movement that typifies the rhythm.

Hundreds of such subtle motions may be orchestrated by each partner during a single dance, and for performer and spectator alike they represent both the joy and the genius of the dance, the gables and porticos built on a solid foundation of skill and ceremony.

SOCIAL DANCERS MAKE FEW distinctions between various dances beyond tempo, rhythm, and the couples' familiarity with the steps. In competition, individual dances are distinguished and classified by various means, and some universal classification will be required before Olympic status is achieved.

The easiest distinction is between Standard/American Smooth and International Latin/American Rhythm dances. The classifications are as representative of their cultural origins as language and cuisine.

International Standard dances include the waltz, tango, Viennese waltz, fox-trot, and quick-step, all danced by men in white tie and women in elaborate gowns. Most facets of International Standard steps were classified by the British in 1924, through the Imperial Society of Teachers of Dancing, and their strict definitions endure today at prestigious events such as the Blackpool Festival.

Other countries followed the British lead, with the exception

Devotees relish the subtleties of various dance styles. The traditional jive may be danced as East Coast swing, West Coast swing, or, in Europe, rock 'n' roll.

of the United States. Here the major dance studios, particularly the Arthur Murray and Fred Astaire organizations, sought a dancing style less formal and restrictive than the one dictated by the British. The quick-step was rejected as too demanding and complex, leaving only four steps in the repertoire, which became known as American Smooth. In any of these steps, at any time, partners may break from the closed position and perform side by side or facing each other, with or without arms or hands joined, synchronized or in solo action.

Costumes reflected this relaxed, permissive style, especially for women. With more and faster spins, gown hemlines were often slit and designed to rise to hip level, revealing full leg lengths. And since the front of a woman's gown is more exposed when dancing in open positions than in closed, bodices of American Smooth dancers tend to be more dramatic and eye-catching.

The advent of U.S. television coverage has made the most of these American Smooth dance characteristics, and many competition performances rival Latin steps for their provocative style and delivery. But the main differences between American Smooth and International Standard remain a matter of emphasis rather than result.

Latin dances are quite a different matter. International Latin dances include five highly distinctive styles: the cha-cha, rumba, samba, paso doble, and jive. The American Rhythm dances retain the cha-cha, rumba, and samba but replace jive with swing, dispose of the paso doble altogether, and may add the mambo, bolero, and merengue. Like the Standard/Smooth distinction, American Rhythm steps are less disciplined than International Latin and more suited for social dancing.

Even individual categories of American Smooth dances are wide open to interpretation. If you dance the swing, you may be asked to choose between East and West Coast style. East Coast swing, danced with no particular alignment, is primarily a rotational step employing a basic triple rhythm. Once the basic rhythm is established, the dancers are free to develop and execute a variety of patterns.

West Coast swing has a flexible alignment structure in which the woman travels back and forth along a determined line, leaving the man in a relatively fixed and centered position. The ideal music for West Coast swing is slower than for East Coast or jive and may include a rolling or "shuffle" beat. Devotees of West Coast swing (or "WC" as they often abbreviate it) admit it is more difficult to master than the East Coast variety but claim it permits more creativity and individual expression.

THE TWO SCHOOLS OF DANCING may be on something of a collision course. Every country except the United States embraces the International styles—disciplined, traditional, and relatively easy to score in competition. But television favors American Smooth and American Latin dances for their color, flamboyance, and unpredictability.

Should dancing achieve Olympic status, it will undoubtedly be based on International steps. But should dancing become embraced by major U.S. television coverage, the network powers will clearly push for American style to generate wider audiences and more intense competition.

Meanwhile, the music plays on. . . .

CHAPTER THREE

Tangos and Tails:
The Standard Dances

AS PERFORMED IN THE International style, the five Standard dances boast diverse origins, rhythms, tempos, and aesthetics but share a basic common feature: they are all danced by a couple—presumably a man and a woman—in the closed position. (American Smooth style permits the couple to break from this position, but it should be seen as a variation of the norm.)

In the closed position, dancers maintain contact between their bodies at five points:

1. The man's left hand holds the woman's right hand.
2. The woman's left hand rests on top of the man's right upper arm. In the tango, she places her hand behind his arm.
3. The man's right hand is placed on the left shoulder blade of the woman.
4. The woman's left elbow rests on the man's right elbow.

As the fox-trot tempo slowed over the years to incorporate more elegant steps, dancers turned to ragtime music for faster, syncopated steps. The result was the quick-step, among the most crowd-pleasing of all dances at competitions.

5. The right side of each partner's rib cage touches the other's.

The woman's upper arms are held horizontally, making it comfortable for her to follow the man's lead and, perhaps more important, creating a stately appearance. The couple moves, for the most part, with erect and fixed torsos, sharing this posture with classical ballet. Both the closed position and classical ballet originated with dances in Western European culture, particularly the royal courts of the seventeenth and eighteenth centuries.

Historians have traced several aspects of the closed position to a series of cultural values dating back to those early days. For example, the woman resting her left elbow on the man's right elbow is probably a vestige of social restraints against women making any sort of advance to a man. Since it was the man's duty to offer himself for a dance, the woman's role was to either accept or reject. While offering himself, the man presented his arm; in accepting, the woman placed her arm upon his. This influenced the posture of the dancers since, to ensure the woman's comfort, the man was required to keep his right shoulder directly above his right hip and his right elbow in front of his shoulder line.

The same social custom influenced the positions of the man's left hand and woman's right hand. Along with offering his right arm to the woman as an invitation to dance, he would present his left hand, palm up. The woman accepted by placing her right hand on his, palm down. While some dance teachers advocate other palm alignments, this traditional position allows each partner to keep the wrists straight and the hands in line with the lower arms. The result is a pleasing, if somewhat formal, line to both partners' bodies.

Another direct result of the man's initiative is his responsibility to lead, and the woman's to follow. More than one feminist (and more than a few doctoral theses) has seized on this aspect of the dance as an example of male domination. For a skilled and experienced dancing couple, however, the choreog-

For International Standard dances, couples maintain the closed position, reflecting the formality of the original eighteenth-century court dances.

raphy and direction of travel, commonly referred to as floorcraft, are shared to a substantial extent. When the man is moving backward, it is the woman who locates any encroaching couple and she may communicate their presence to her partner, avoiding an embarrassing collision.

Other criticisms of the closed position are more specific. Why, for example, do the partners not gaze into each other's eyes as they dance? To do so would seriously inhibit their floorcraft, of course, but there are other good reasons for avoiding a direct alignment between the partners' heads. Offsetting the bodies in this way staggers the position of the feet. This avoids (or should) the partners' feet arriving in the same position on the floor at exactly the same time—an inevitable occurrence if the man and woman are perfectly in line with each other unless they move in lockstep.

Dance teachers offer other, perhaps more frivolous explanations. In social dancing, the couple inevitably make small talk as they dance, and it makes more sense to talk into your partner's ear than into his or her nose. Another teacher responds: "If you look straight at your partner, you're left with only peripheral vision to apply your floorcraft. Since I know how good-looking my partner is, I can leave her/him in my peripheral vision and use direct vision to spot oncoming traffic."

Some dances require other locations for body contact, especially at the advanced levels. During spins in waltzes or the quickstep, most experienced dancers look for hip contact as a way of uniting each partner's motions through the intricate steps.

None of this, of course, becomes effective when the couples break during an American Smooth step. But even during these dances, the couples inevitably begin with or return to a closed position during the dance, and the same guidelines apply.

THE VIENNESE WALTZ IS ROOTED in the most ancient of social dances, tracing its origins back to the twelfth and thirteenth centuries in the opinion of some historians. Medieval dancers in Bavaria performed the "Nachantz" in this period, around the same time as Parisians were stepping to the volta, an import from Provence. *Volta* means "the turn" in Italian, suggesting that the dance arrived in Provence by way of Italy.

The singular characteristic of the nachantz and the volta is their rhythm. Both are performed to music with three beats to the bar, which creates both difficulties and charm. Two beats to the bar is more natural to humans, because we walk on two feet. By the same token, four beats to the bar is more natural to animals and to ourselves, as the steady, soothing rhythm of a trotting horse can attest.

With three beats to the bar—*one* two three, *one* two three—the first step in each bar of music is taken with the opposite foot (*left* right left, *right* left right). This presents a challenge to novice dancers, but also produces a romantic lilt to the partners' bodies as they move.

By the sixteenth century the volta had become a popular dance in the royal courts of Western Europe, although it was far more boisterous than today's Viennese waltz. One variation involved the man holding the woman by her waist while the woman placed her right arm on the man's shoulder. Her left arm held her skirt, a necessary precaution because the man routinely lifted the woman by placing his left thigh beneath her right thigh. The close embrace used by volta dancers scandalized the Church, which persuaded Louis XIII of France to ban it from his court.

In the middle of the eighteenth century the first music composed especially for *Waltzen* (meaning "to revolve" in German) appeared, setting off another wave of moral outrage, this time in Austria. A pamphlet published in 1797 declared its entire premise in its title: *Proof That Waltzing Is a Main Source of Weakness of the Body and Mind of Our Generation.*

This, naturally, served only to build its popularity, especially in Vienna. Soon large dance halls were constructed to meet the demands of Viennese waltzers. The Apollo, opened in 1808, was apparently large enough to accommodate six thousand dancers. By the end of the century, compositions by the Strauss family (Johann I, Johann II, and Josef) launched the Viennese waltz into a near-craze that swept across Europe and took Britain by

The Viennese waltz epitomizes all the romantic appeal of International Standard dances: grace, elegance, and illusory romance.

storm. Still, an aura of disrepute hovered over the Viennese waltz for many years. A book on manners and social behavior published by an Englishwoman in 1833 reluctantly accepted the idea of married women participating in the waltz but declared it "a dance of too loose character for maidens to perform."

Through the nineteenth century, British upper classes considered dancing an important skill to be learned by anyone aspiring to a respectable social position. When dancing migrated across the Atlantic to North America, it achieved egalitarian status, losing some respectability in the process. All classes of Americans pursued dancing in halls where alcohol was served, and soon the elegant waltz was being denounced as evil by organized religion.

As late as 1894, a "reformed" dance master named T. A. Faulkner published *From the Ball-Room to Hell*, tracing the path leading directly from a young girl's first dance lesson to the loss of her virtue. The author concludes, with questionable deduction, that "two-thirds of all girls who are ruined fall through the influence of dancing," and that a study he conducted among brothels in the Los Angeles area identified 163 out of 200 women who blamed their "ruin" on dancing schools and ballrooms.[1]

Today, the Viennese waltz is danced at a brisk tempo of about 180 beats per minute. Turns and spins still constitute a major portion of its character, sprinkled among a change of steps, hesitations, and hovers. In competition, it is important for the partners, particularly the women, to express sheer joy and delight.

THE MODERN WALTZ DEVELOPED from regional variations of the *Waltzen* in Germany and Austria. In an area of upper Austria called Landl ob der Enns, townsfolk created a dance in 3/4 time featuring complex underarm turns and animated hopping, slapping, and stamping steps. Thanks to its place of origin, this became known as the Landler. With time, the dancers discarded the heavy shoes worn when performing the original steps, replacing them with light footwear and adding a few gliding and rotating motions from the Viennese waltz. To accommodate the Landler's underarm turns and other intricate motions, the dance was performed at a much more leisurely pace than the Viennese waltz.

Around 1870, a similar variation of the Viennese waltz evolved in the United States. Called the Boston, this version of the waltz was performed with the dancers placing their hands on each other's hips. It retained the turning figures of the original waltz form, adding new motions such as dips and spins.

Inevitably, the Landler and the Boston were combined, probably in England soon after Queen Victoria's death. Keeping the closed position of the Viennese waltz, the dancers took advantage of the slower tempo to add new figures such as extra syncopated beats and slow "picture" steps. When England's legendary Victor Sylvester won the world championship in 1922, the waltz consisted of little more than a right turn, a left turn, and a change of direction—or fewer steps than a beginner learns today. Within a few years of Sylvester's victory, the basic movements of the waltz were established as step-side-close, which lent the dancers more opportunity to add new elements such as spin turns and pivots.

The wider variation in speeds and motion also gave the dance a more complex, less predictable appearance than the faster, more exuberant Viennese version, adding to its widespread popularity as the modern waltz.

THE TANGO IS THE VICTIM OF PERHAPS more confused and stereotyped interpretation than any other dance, especially in North America and Britain. The roots of these misconceptions may lie in its unique position as the only Standard or American Smooth dance without an Anglo-Saxon heritage. Or perhaps certain formalities of the dance leave it more vulnerable to parody than others. Recent movies, such as *True Lies*, with Arnold Schwarzenegger showing surprising grace, and Al Pacino proving the blind can dance in *Scent of a Woman*, are only the latest in Hollywood's treatment of the tango in a derisive, superficial manner.

◀ **SLOW WALTZ**   The most blatantly romantic of all the Standard dance steps, the slow waltz features graceful moves such as the *Hinge Line,* in which the woman seems to float in the man's arms with an expression of sheer delight on her face. Note the man's full extension of his back leg and left hand held high.

FOX-TROT   Despite its popularity among social dancers, the fox-trot is considered the most difficult of all Standard dances to perform successfully at the competition level. Many steps are performed on the toes, and the woman places her hand under the man's upper arm—an important device to guide her partner when he is moving backward. ▶

◀ **VIENNESE WALTZ**   More energetic than the slow waltz, the Viennese style features the *Fleckerel,* a continuous rotation on the spot, usually performed in the center of the dance floor. The smallest details receive the most rapt attention: the man's strict vertical posture, the woman's placement of her left hand, the careful intertwining of the fingers.

◀ TANGO   Thanks to its somewhat tawdry origins, the tango demands an attitude sharply in contrast with other Standard dances. Links or "head snaps" are an integral part of every performance. The partners avoid direct eye contact, and their facial expressions—the man domineering, the woman haughty and disdainful—mask any enjoyment.

QUICK-STEP   The Standard dance equivalent to the ▶ jive, the quick-step is energetic and exuberant. Often, the dancers hop in place, waiting for an opening on the floor or a break in the music to resume their progression around the floor, and partners position themselves for brisk motions.

◀ AMERICAN SMOOTH   Less restricted than International Standard, American Smooth dancers frequently break from the closed position to improvise steps during any of the prescribed dances. Here they remain in the open position, but they could separate entirely and dance side by side.

To the uninitiated, the tango suggests parody and affectation. But true tango adherents love its symbolism and delight in its unique character.

Those who understand the tango view it as an exotic, provocative, challenging, and athletically demanding dance, especially if they have been fortunate enough to witness the touring company of *Forever Tango*. Still, its origins and development remain hazy, and its most elegant aspects are performed correctly by only a limited number of dancers.

Some historians trace the tango back to the ancient light-spirited Spanish flamenco dance of the same name. This may be true, but others point out that the Latin *tangere*—"to touch"—may be just as likely a source of the name. The Spanish colonialists brought flamenco with them to South America, where, like all colonial imports, it soon melded with other influences and emerged as something quite different.

The *tangano* (a verbal imitation of the sound of drumbeats) is also a likely ancestor of the modern tango. African slaves performed the tangano in the New World, where it merged with the Spanish flamenco and traditional native dances. By the late nineteenth century it had become popular in the slums of Buenos Aires. Dancers in the barrios called it *baile con corte*, or "dance with a rest," referring to the manner in which the dancers would suddenly pause for a beat or two before resuming their progress. The *baile con corte* was performed to a two-beat rhythm more reminiscent of a modern polka than the tango we know today.

With the arrival of a folk dance from Cuba called the *habanera*, the Buenos Aires dancers blended it with their *baile con corte*, producing a new step often identified as the *milonga*.

In contrast with the contemporary tango in any of its variations, the *milonga* was a very soft private dance emphasizing leg movements, but it soon transformed into a dramatic theatrical performance with sudden head snaps, erect torsos, and arrogant, almost disdainful facial expressions.

The tango's earliest, most enthusiastic performers were found in the brothels and back alleys of Buenos Aires. Massive immigration to Argentina in the 1880s brought scores of new arrivals from Europe and Africa, many of them lonely outcasts who gravitated to the cheap bars along the docks where they sought love and companionship, no matter how brief or tawdry.

They danced to music based upon the relentless tribal rhythms of African slaves, played against Spanish laments influenced by native folk songs. Regardless of the influences, the basic emotions expressed by the music were passion and sorrow over strict rhythms laid down by piano and bass. The melody was usually provided by performers on the *bandoneon*, an accordionlike instrument from Germany which, in the hands of a true Argentine tango player, creates a wailing sense of melancholy and alienation.

Early tango music was generally regarded as obscene, like the dance it inspired. Even many tango song titles were scandalous, referring to underworld characters fighting over the favors or even outright ownership of a woman.

Certainly this was the message delivered by *Forever Tango*: the man exerting his power over the woman, who defiantly refuses to surrender on the dance floor. Some historians suggest the exotic nature of the dance as performed by Rudolph Valentino and Beatrice Dominguez in the 1921 film *The Four Horsemen of the Apocalypse* set the tone for the dance.

Valentino's embrace of the tango, with all its sensual suggestions, ignited Paris society. Not surprisingly, church disapproval soon followed. At least one French bishop declared that anyone who danced the outrageous tango was endangering the sanctity of the holy sacraments. A New York doctor named Boheme claimed to discover a new disease which he dubbed "the Tango-foot," and for which he no doubt proffered a cure.

The tango, in light of its ribald origins and mannerisms, became an obvious target for critics. It was left to Vernon and Irene Castle to popularize the dance for "respectable" citizens. They were married, sophisticated, and solidly middle-class, and they adapted its most appealing aspects in a distinctive dance that, in a manner of speaking, "side-stepped" any obvious references to its unsavory origins. For the Castles, tawdry seduction was the furthest thing from their minds when performing the tango. As Irene Castle wrote in her memoirs: "If Vernon had looked into my eyes with smoldering passion during the tango, we both would have burst out laughing."[2]

The Castles, perhaps more gifted dancers than Astaire and Rogers, thus established a tone still followed to this day by ballroom dancers and DanceSport participants. The dance is taken seriously; the underlying passion is not.

When the tango's popularity blossomed in Paris during the thirties its sudden leg and hip movements, typical of the Argentine version, were replaced with quick motions of the dancers' heads and a staccato action as the couple progressed across the floor. This divergence between the dance's Argentine origins and its Western European adaptation remains in the existence of two distinct forms of the dance—or perhaps three, considering both International and American Smooth steps.

The Argentine tango is not codified, making it difficult to judge and assess its performance in organized competition. Still, it retains a dedicated following among dancers who consider it a rival to the quick-step for finesse and athleticism. Devotees of the Argentine tango seem attracted by its complexity and may be inspired to play out certain aspects of cultural fantasies or psychological motivations—strictly for fun, of course. One New York ballroom expert put it this way: "The Argentine tango tells the story of a gangster and his woman, and the woman hates the man, even though they are lovers. You pretend for an evening, then you go to a restaurant and eat Chinese."

Teachers of the Argentine tango often suggest their students imagine walking barefoot across hot sand in order to create a sense of lightness in the foot movements. Basic steps of the Argentine tango include figure eights, turns, and walking, with the addition of dramatic pauses, quick steps, syncopations, leg hooks, and back kicks. Tango masters emphasize and exaggerate these motions for theatrical effect, but they stem from the same roots, the same traditions, and the same fantasies.

In competitive ballroom dancing, the motions are fixed within a syllabus and the dancers move with more regal grace than the passionate Argentine performers. Those choosing the American Modern style frequently break from the closed

position, nullifying the clutching embrace exemplifying the roots of the dance.

Head snaps are a staple of the tango in all its styles, and when performed incorrectly they appear either silly and pretentious or as a parody of the tango, like carrying a rose in one's teeth. Snaps are performed during an abrupt change in direction known as a "link." Head snaps are communicated from the man to his partner through "contra body movement," a sudden straightening of the body which signals the woman, through rib cage and arm motion, to perform the link.

Why head snaps at all? One explanation is to see the tango as a stalking dance, the ballroom equivalent of a cat approaching its prey. The dance partners must move without seeming to move, and the head snaps are the logical method of suddenly reversing one's view. Like all singular aspects of dance, when done well it is captivating; when done poorly, it is mystifying at best.

A tongue-in-cheek view of the three tango styles has been provided by one dance observer:

> The tango is like stages of a marriage. The American Modern Tango is like the beginning of a love affair, when you are both very romantic and on your best behavior. The Argentine Tango is when you are in the heat of things and all kinds of emotions are flying: passion, anger, humor. The International Standard Tango is like the end of the marriage, when you are staying together for the sake of the children.[3]

THE SLOW FOX-TROT IS OFTEN erroneously associated with the walking pace of the doglike animal in its name. Actually, the dance originated with Harry Fox, who introduced it in the 1913 Broadway show *Ziegfeld Follies.* Vernon and Irene Castle embellished the basic steps into a nightclub performance soon afterward, and the fox-trot was suddenly a sensation.

Fox derived his dance from a faster Victorian-era dance called either the one-step or two-step. Whatever its name, the dance was identical, based on one step per beat or, since the music was

The tango includes "head snaps," performed during sudden changes in direction called "links," which are a carryover from the tango's origins as a stalking dance. Done well, links are captivating; performed poorly, they are merely perplexing.

played in 2/4 time, two steps to the bar. The tempo was sprightly—more than 160 beats per minute—and the movements were apparently quite jerky as a result.

Much of the fox-trot's early appeal was based on the foot position. Victorian-era dances called for each partner's feet to be turned outward, but with the fox-trot the feet remained parallel. To young dancers, this represented a rebellion of sorts, and undoubtedly added to its popularity.

By the end of World War I, the dance had been slowed considerably (to about 120 beats per minute) and the trotting steps discarded in favor of smooth, gliding movements. By that time, the dance was based on four key steps: walks, three-steps, a slow walk, and a slow spin-turn. During the 1920s a number of now-common figures were added, including the feather-step and change of direction.

Perhaps more than any other ballroom dance, the fox-trot remains the most popular social dance activity, thanks to its very natural motion and the wide variety of interpretations available to the dancers. Most of its movements derive naturally from normal walking patterns, adding to its easy accessibility for beginners, and its smooth character is much more appealing to novices than, say, the tango. Yet the fox-trot is also acknowledged as the most difficult dance to master at the competitive level, the one dance that quickly separates the masters from the also-rans.

THE QUICK-STEP OWES ITS BEGINNINGS to two quite different developments: the demand for slower fox-trot tempos in search of smooth gliding motions, and the influence of ragtime music on dancing.

Ragtime grew in parallel with jazz, an African-American music phenomenon that rose from a complex set of roots, including American folk songs, African tribal rhythms, and brass band music. The common elements in ragtime were the intense syncopation and strong rhythmic drive, best demonstrated in the music of Scott Joplin, ragtime's most musically trained and popular composer.

The syncopation and rhythm of ragtime cried out for new

dance patterns, and in response a number of them emerged to great enthusiasm and popularity, including the shimmy, the black bottom, and the Charleston. This last was said to have originated with dock workers in the port of Charleston, who performed a vigorous round dance to ragtime rhythms. A 1922 Broadway review produced by George White introduced the dance to northern white audiences, and when a touring production of the Ziegfeld Follies carried the dance to major cities throughout the United States, the Charleston craze began. Soon all of Europe was caught up in the mania, thanks to the arrival of Josephine Baker in Paris. Performed at 200 or 240 beats per minute, the Charleston was danced with wild swinging arms and side-kicks, causing many ballrooms to ban it. Others displayed notices saying "PCQ," which meant Please Charleston Quietly.

Slowing the fox-trot to a more sedate tempo left a vacuum for more exuberant dancers, who began combining music and steps of the older, faster fox-trot with figures from the Charleston and black bottom. The result was the quick-step, the most joyful and high-spirited dance in the Standard repertoire. Retaining the progressive motions of the original fox-trot, the quick-step added the hops, skips, and kicks of the Charleston into a dance that remains popular with performers and audiences alike.

CHAPTER FOUR

Mambos and Morals:
The Latin Dances

WE REFER TO THEM AS LATIN dances, yet in every case but one, the unifying element among them is not Latin-based at all. It is African.[1]

Latin defines the culture thanks to the predominance of Romance languages—French, Spanish, and Portuguese—in countries that inspired the dances. But without the power and inspiration of African rhythms, none of these steps, except for the paso doble, would exist.

Of the five dances in the Latin repertoire, three originated in the Caribbean and South America, one in the United States, and one in Spain. The cha-cha, rumba, and samba all represent a fusion of music and dances by indigenous New World tribes, Spanish and Portuguese colonialists, and West African natives imported as slaves.

Dance played a major role in all these cultures, and when the three influences melded into one they generated even more enthusiasm and celebration. This made the colonial establishment decidedly uncomfortable. Like their contemporaries in

Latin dances evolved from a variety of cultures, primarily African, Cuban, and South American. They retain their raw sensuality in attitude, motions, and especially costumes.

Western Europe, New World governors and church leaders felt threatened by the dances and responded accordingly.

In 1569 Luis de Velasco, viceroy of Mexico, angrily ordered the Aztec Calendar Stone to be buried because African slaves and natives insisted on dancing around it. When the slaves and natives found other suitable locations and occasions for dancing, Velasco went further, decreeing that dancing could occur only on Sundays and feast days between noon and 6:00 P.M.

Poor Velasco. He might as well have ordered the tide to stop flowing as persuade his subjects to stop dancing. His restrictions inspired a new round of fusion between African and native music, producing rhythms more powerful than those he tried to suppress, all of it blossoming into a cultural movement called Creole. To this was added the influence of sophisticated European dances drifting into Latin America with the colonists, and the explosive popularity of the *Contradanza Habanera* from Cuba. Suddenly, dancing for Latin Americans was as natural, and almost as necessary, as eating and breathing.

Latin American music has been transformed over and over again into highly complex rhythms. The melodies are heavily syncopated, irresistibly compelling, and physically demanding on the dancers' response. In a slow fox-trot, the rhythm beats at a steady four-to-the-bar pace, emphasizing even the mildest off-beat syncopation. But Latin American dance music (virtually *all* Latin American music is composed and played for dancing) involves a wide array of syncopation, with heavily accented notes falling almost anywhere according to the style of dance for which the music has been written. Dancers remain acutely attuned to differences between the various rhythms, instantly identifying them by name and creating dance figures that mirror the passion and exuberance of the music. Few musical events can rival a Latin dance festival for its ability to touch the hearts and souls of performers and spectators alike, generating spontaneous cheers of approval and admiration from all sides.

THE SAMBA REFLECTS THE MANY differences in cultural roots and influences that give Latin music and dance its

The samba originated with African slaves transported to Brazil by the Portuguese. Embraced and performed by personalities as wide-ranging as Fred Astaire, Carmen Miranda, and Britain's Princess Margaret, the dance retains its expressive joy tinged with melancholia.

multifaceted character. Its home is Brazil, the only Portuguese-speaking country in Latin America, and while the distinction may appear minor to North Americans and Europeans, the dance's birthplace helped create a unique and distinctive dance culture.

The Portuguese brought their African slaves from Angola and the Congo, regions that boasted their own unique dances including the *catarete, embolada,* and *batuque.* All dancing was considerable sinful by the Church, but these represented a major descent into depravity primarily because they involved the touching of navels between male and female dancers.

The embolada was a joyful dance about a cow that wears balls on its horns to prevent it from injuring others. In the batuque, which may have its origins in a wedding or fertility celebration, the couple danced steps similar to the Charleston within a circle of other dancers who urged them on with shouts, hand-clapping, and steps of their own.

Eventually the batuque grew so popular that it achieved the elevated status of all exuberant dances of its time: it was banned by King Manuel I, which of course simply encouraged its refinement out of sight of the authorities.

By the mid-1800s the batuque gained respectability, and when the Carnival steps of the Copacabana influenced it, the dance was soon embraced by upper-class Rio society. Like other privileged colonialists, members of Rio society followed the lead of their European forebears in many ways, and in Europe all dancing was performed in the closed position, man and woman facing each other, the man leading, the woman following.

The new dance needed a new name, and around 1885 it was being referred to as the *zemba queca, zembo* being a colloquial description of a child born of African and native parents. (It may also have reflected an ancient Brazilian folk dance called the *semba,* resembling even older steps and figures traced back to Angolan Africa.) Eventually the zemba/semba/samba grew, influenced by the *maxixe,* yet another Brazilian round dance performed as a two-step to Cuban music.

Something about the samba—its expression of joy tinged

with melancholia—appealed to Europe and North America, an appeal that exploded into popularity when Fred Astaire and Ginger Rogers performed a variation of the samba dubbed the *carioca* in the 1933 film *Flying Down to Rio*. Carmen Miranda, banana-bunch hat and all, further stimulated the craze when she gyrated to the carioca in *That Night in Rio* and other film productions.

The final blessing arrived in the mid-1950s, when Princess Margaret was seen dancing the samba with much enthusiasm on numerous occasions, adding a luster of British royal approval to the dance and raising interest in Latin dancing generally.

While the world beyond Brazil absorbed the samba as a clearly defined series of steps and figures, the dance grew more complex and interpretative in its homeland. During Rio's *Carnaval*, samba dancers may perform any of a series of dances, all related in their rhythm and tempo but subtly different in their execution. To the uninitiated, they are all the samba; to the discerning eye of a true *Carioca* the dancers may be performing the *baion* or the *marcha* or one of several other variations on the national dance.

One reason for the samba's steady popularity beyond Brazil may be its generally wide range of interpretation, even though its moves have been formally codified for competition purposes. The modern samba features a flat torso position for the dancers, who keep their weight well forward on the toes and insert a pelvic tilt action on the half-beat between steps, a characteristic known as the "samba tic." The hip movement is difficult to master for some dancers, but without it the samba loses much of its effect and appeal.

A curious fact: no one from Brazil, the birthplace of the samba, has scored well at top-level world dance championships. Nor would they be likely to without extensive training by a professional-level coach, preferably British. The Brazilian method may be authentic, but it is not authorized or standardized for international ballroom performances.

THE RUMBA, A SLOW, SENSUAL DANCE, is often referred to as a dance of love. One interpretation suggests that it represents the beginning of the love experience, with each partner tempting the other to go further, producing a provocative blend of aggression and retreat.

Once again the rumba's origins can be traced directly back to Africa, in this case members of various peoples who were

Outrageous costumes and suggestive moves are defining features of this "hot-blooded" dance style.

brought as slaves to Cuba during the seventeenth century. Unlike the samba, which tends to emphasize foot movements, the rumba focused more attention on body movements performed to the beat of complex cross-rhythms provided by beating on pots, pans, and bottles.

Why *rumba*? Take your pick from a number of possible name sources. Cuban dance bands in the early 1800s were referred to

In the paso doble, the man is a bullfighter and the woman is his cape (the bull, hopefully, is nowhere to be seen). By focusing exclusively on character, the paso doble leaves little room for improvisation.

as *rumboso* (flashy, showy) *orquestas*. In Spanish, *rumbo* means route, *rumba* means a pile of trash, and of course rum is the Caribbean's indigenous liquor.

Whatever the source of its name, the rumba soon became the most popular dance in Cuba. Rural dancers performed it not as a means of seduction but as a pantomime of barnyard animals, for exhibition rather than participation. Town folk adapted these steps along with some peculiar figures still seen today; the *cucaracha* imitated the motion of stomping on a cockroach, and in the spot turn dancers imitated the action of walking around the circumference of a cartwheel.

The popularity of the rumba inspired music written especially for the dance, such as "La Paloma," first heard in Cuba during the mid-1860s.

Still, the rumba remained a somewhat primitive dance until it appeared in the United States during the dance-crazy 1930s, when it was blended with the cheerful *guaracha* and the Cuban *bolero*. In this version of the rumba, dancers break on the first beat of each bar, but when British dance teacher Pierre Lavelle visited Havana soon after World War II he discovered the Cubans breaking on the second beat. Along with names for rumba dance figures he acquired from Cuban dance master Pepe Rivera, Lavelle inserted this into a syllabus for the international Cuban rumba.

According to some, the international rumba represents a more sensual dance than the American version. International dancers merely shift their weight from one foot to the other on the first beat of each bar. This is the strongest beat of the music, but only the hips move, emphasizing the pelvic region. Actual steps take place on beats two, three, and four at a slow tempo of about 115 beats per minute. Actions on the half-beat include straightening the knee, transferring weight, and performing turns. Like the samba, the dancers keep their weight well forward, almost on tiptoe.

Although the rumba is celebrated as the dance of love, it is most interesting and successful when the partners express something more than peaceful romance. The top practitioners

The cha-cha, a cheeky, playful, and flirtatious dance that originated in Cuba, demands strong hip movement while the dancers keep their weight well forward.

insist that partners perform all the other aspects of a love story, including passion, desire, jealousy, hate, and pain. When a superbly trained and inspired couple dances the rumba, they act out a personal and complex love story—the man turns the woman toward him, she turns away only to turn back once more and give herself to him before he rejects her, et cetera.

Understanding these roles and actions as part of the dance dialogue enriches the enjoyment for the spectator and elevates the dance to something beyond the partners' individual motions.

THE PASO DOBLE IS ONE OF MANY folk dances portraying various facets of Spanish life, in this case the actions of a bullfight. First-time observers of the dance may assume the dancers represent the matador and the bull, but in fact they depict the torero and his cape.

Danced to characteristic two-beat march music played for the procession into the ring—*paso doble* means two-step in Spanish—the dance became popular in Paris during the 1930s among the salon set, which accounts for the French names applied to many of its steps. Of all the Latin dances, the paso doble is danced by the fewest number of participants, due probably to its formalities and the demands it places on the dancers' understanding of Spanish culture.

In competition, the paso doble is danced with the chest held high, the shoulders positioned wide and down, and the head inclined forward. (One teacher of the paso doble reminds his students to "Keep watching that bull!") It is a somewhat awkward posture for dancing at first, but essential to convey the challenge of the bullfighter (and his "cape") to the animal. Body weight is kept forward, though not to the extent of the samba and rumba. Many of the steps require the dancer to lead with the heel, so frequent weight shifts are necessary.

The most popular music selected for the paso doble is the "España Cani," or "Spanish Gypsy Dance." Its three crescendos provide opportunities for the dancers to strike dramatic poses at these points, elevating the theatrical nature of the dance even further.

Of the five International Latin steps, the paso doble is the last to be attempted by beginners. The dance leaves less room for improvisation than other Latin steps, and couples must work at filling the character roles demanded for the performance to succeed.

THE CHA-CHA, PERHAPS THE MOST exciting dance in the Latin group, is also both the newest of the International Latin/American Rhythm dances and the most international in nature.

The jive is the only "Latin" dance with a North American heritage, and it has spun off a range of styles including swing, boogie-woogie, bebop, rock, twist, disco, and the hustle.

◀ **SAMBA**   Associated with Carman Miranda ever since the 1933 movie *Flying Down to Rio*, the Samba affords perhaps the widest range of interpretation by the dancers. Mastering the "samba tic"—a pelvic tilt on the half-beat between steps—is the biggest challenge in mastering the dance.

RUMBA   Its history traces from African slaves who ▶ settled in Cuba, where their music and dancing melded with Colonial Spanish and local native steps. Top dancers use the rumba to act out aspects of love, from passion and desire through jealousy, hate, and pain.

◀ **PASO DOBLE**   The man is the matador, the woman is his cape, and the steps tend to be less open to improvisation than other Latin dances because the partners must remain in character. Dramatic poses, as seen here, are cued to crescendos in the music—usually the "Spanish Gypsy Dance."

◀ CHA-CHA Happy, carefree and flirtatious, the cha-cha is often danced with the woman "teasing" the man—presenting herself as a desirable object before dancing away and tempting him to pursue her. A step is taken with each beat of the music; the knee straightens on the half-beat, producing strong hip movements.

JIVE Always the last in a five-dance Latin series, the ▶ jive is also the most physically demanding. Since the days of the black bottom and the jitterbug, each succeeding generation has developed its own variation, but the powerful two-beat rhythm remains constant—as does the youthful exuberance.

◀ SWING Dance competitions in the United States may feature this variation of the jive. East Coast swing, danced at a slower tempo than jive, retains the feeling of a fifties' high school dance; the West Coast version, performed to a "shuffle" beat, often positions the dancers side by side. Both styles are more relaxed than the sometimes frantic jive steps.

Swing began as a modified jive, but both East Coast and West Coast variations have exploded in popularity, each with its own adherents.

Like its sister steps, the samba and rumba, the cha-cha's roots are deeply embedded in West African rhythms heavily influenced by Spanish colonialist culture and native dances. But the cha-cha owes much of its heritage to English dance teacher Pierre Lavelle, who visited Cuba in 1952. In the Havana nightclubs he noticed that the rumba was often danced with the addition of extra beats, creating a staccato rhythm and a good deal of freestyle motions by the dancers. Music for the dance tended to emphasize five beats within a 4/4 bar: *one, two, one-two-three, one, two, one-two-three,* et cetera.

On his return to England, Lavelle formalized many of the figures he had witnessed and began teaching the dance as the "Cha-cha-cha." Why such a name? Like other dances, no simple answer exists and there is no evidence that Lavelle either heard the dance referred to by this name in Cuba or concocted the name on his own. In Spanish the word *chacha* means nursemaid, and *chachar* means to chew coca leaves. And of course another popular dance of the time, the *guaracha,* may have been yet one more inspiration.

The cha-cha (most people prefer to drop the third "cha" from Lavelle's original "cha-cha-cha") may be as deeply rooted in the mambo as the rumba. Around the time Lavelle was teaching his new dance to enthusiastic students in England, the mambo burst out of Haiti, where it occupied a role in certain voodoo rituals. The two words that best describe the mambo are "hot" and "steamy." Soon after the cha-cha's introduction one dance expert dismissed it as just a slower mambo with a *guiro* rhythm, the *guiro* being a dried gourd rubbed with a serrated stick to produce a clicking sort of syncopation.

The wide popularity and distinctive nature of the cha-cha has produced a special interpretation often (but not always) applied by judges in dance competitions. Without question, the cha-cha is a carefree, "cheeky" dance suggesting a party atmosphere. Some teachers and interpreters go further, suggesting it represents a flirtation by the woman. Certainly the cha-cha's happy, staccato rhythm produces a light and playful dance, but many observers suggest the partners—as part of the "flirtation"

game—cease their rapid steps and slow down from time to time.

Dancing at about 120 beats per minute, cha-cha performers take a step on each beat, producing a strong hip movement as the knee straightens on the offbeat, while keeping their weight well forward.

THE JIVE, THE ONLY "LATIN" DANCE with a North American heritage, owes its rhythmic drive to the African slave trade, although it appears that Florida's Seminole Indians had an influence as well.

The word *jive* had various slang meanings among Afro-Americans in the mid-1800s. To "jive" was to speak insultingly of someone, or to talk boastfully with great exaggeration. The word also referred to gaudy merchandise, marijuana, and love-making, although it's difficult to determine if these definitions arose out of the dance or vice-versa.

In any case, jive was originally a two-part dance in which couples first formed a solemn procession while dressed in their finest clothes, then performed an energetic display dance to syncopated two-beat music. This gave rise to two terms most historians agree are associated with jive's origin: cakewalk and ragtime. In jive dance competitions, the prize was frequently a cake, so the dance itself was referred to as a cakewalk. Black slang also referred to clothes as "rags," so dressing in your best clothes meant putting on your best "rags." The music you danced to was also syncopated or "ragged" in style, leading to "ragtime."

After the Union victory in the U.S. Civil War, little if any cultural exchange took place between white Americans and newly freed Afro-Americans, especially in music and dance. The death of Britain's Prince Albert in 1861 made its influence felt in the United States, at least among the upper classes. In the fashion of the times, as dictated by British culture, they danced dour, stiff, formalized steps to music of a similar demeanor.

Meanwhile, jive grew more experimental and enthusiastic. Black music and culture began moving north from its birthplace in the South to the cramped urban ghettos of New York and Chicago. Eventually its influence would prove enormous, culminating in jazz and changing the nature of popular music forever.

Perhaps triggered by the death of Queen Victoria in 1901 or simply responding to a pent-up demand for more gaiety and freedom, Americans in the early years of the twentieth century grew hungry for simple, lighthearted music and dancing. They began turning to a bewildering array of often silly steps, most of them derived from Afro-American dances but carefully homogenized to remove anything overly sensual. The dances were christened with appropriately frivolous names: Yankee tangle, Texas rag, fanny bump, funky butt, the squat, the itch, the grind, and the mooche. Some dances were awarded animal names suggestive of their rural roots or pantomime qualities: lame duck, horse trot, grizzly bear, crab step, eagle rock, buzzard lope, turkey trot, kangaroo dip, fish walk, and bunny hug.

All were performed to music that borrowed heavily from Afro-American culture, stressing the second and fourth beat of a bar and with limited syncopation. Irving Berlin's 1910 hit "Alexander's Ragtime Band" is a superb example of white music retaining superficial aspects of more powerful Afro-American culture. Dancers would walk, rock, swoop, spin, bounce, and sway to Berlin's hit song, avoiding the closed position because it was considered indecent in the context of this music.

Ragtime grew both more complex and more popular. By the 1920s ragtime's successor was known as jazz, and the new music began influencing Broadway and vaudeville. *George White's Scandals*, a 1926 Broadway hit, introduced the black bottom to an audience already enthusiastically doing the Charleston. The following year the Lindy hop appeared, named for Charles Lindbergh's solo flight across the Atlantic.

Since then, the dance has progressed in many directions but always retaining its frantic motion in response to the same powerful two-beat, or "backbeat," rhythm. The popularity of jive—once referred to as the jitterbug—has been powered, like most of the other Latin steps, by a sense of rebellion against authority. In the case of the samba and rumba, the Church and government represented disapproving powers. By the Roaring Twenties, however, the strongest disapproval was directed by parents and older adults against a dance which they claimed was not only decadent but disruptive to other dancers. Many dance hall managers tried banning the jive because, as a nonprogressive dance, it disturbed other dancers moving in a counterclockwise motion around the dance floor.

Their efforts, of course, only served to strengthen the

dedication of young dancers to the new steps, often pushing the dance figures to new lengths—or, more accurately, new heights, with some male dancers propelling their partners into vertical back-flips. Thus, jive branched into new variations with every succeeding generation, producing swing, boogie-woogie, bebop, rock, twist, disco, and hustle.

Jive, as danced in competition, incorporates basic steps such as a quick syncopated *chasse* (side, close, side) to each side in turn. All steps are taken on the toes, forcing the weight well forward, and the hips are moved on the half-beat. The various steps and figures place enormous demands on the dancers' athletic abilities and physical condition, demands which are heightened because it is always placed last in a series of five demanding International dances (four basic dances in the American Rhythm sequence).

SWING (EAST COAST AND WEST COAST) and *rock 'n' roll* (the dance, not the music genre) are offshoots of jive. Each dance retains its own adherents and continues to evolve as dancers experiment with the steps and possibilities.

East Coast swing (ECS) is danced to slower, more earthy music than traditional jive. Often described as a spot dance (as opposed to a progressive dance, in which the couples move around the floor), ECS features lots of spins and turns with the partners facing each other. And while ECS is excited in its motions, the moves are rarely sexual and the feeling is reminiscent of mid-fifties high school kids dancing in the gymnasium.

West Coast swing (WCS) is performed to music with a "shuffle" beat, and the dancers are often positioned side-by-side. Fans of this dance claim it is much more relaxed than similar versions of jive, leaving more room for improvisation by the women dancers.

Rock 'n' roll, as danced in Europe, borders on the extremes of athleticism. Both partners kick high—above the horizontal—requiring them to position themselves carefully to avoid injury. Female partners are routinely tossed in the air above their male partners' heads, looking as much like Midwest American college cheerleaders as dancers.

More variations of jive are performed than any other style of dancing. Many of the styles are limited to one area of the United States, and major distinctions between them may rest more in the dancers' imaginations than anywhere else. In southern California, couples perform the *Balboa*, a very fast eight-beats-to-the-bar dance, usually performed in the closed position and consisting entirely of footwork. Florida dancers perform the *beach bop*, a circular style of smooth swing danced to early rhythm-and-blues music. Along the Carolina coastline you may encounter the *Carolina shag*, danced to shuffle-beat music in a laid-back style permitting the man to perform most of the fancy footwork, mirrored by his partner. St. Louis boasts both the *imperial*, a variation of East Coast swing, and its own version of the shag; in New Orleans they favor the *Jamaica*, another East Coast swing derivative; dancers in Dallas and elsewhere in Texas practice the *push* when they're not line-dancing; and on and on.

WITH THE EXCEPTION OF THE PASO DOBLE, all Latin steps represent in one manner or another a form of youthful rebellion against older authority and cultural restriction. Jive and its many offspring continue to express alienation by young adults who insist on rejecting "acceptable" restrictions on public behavior.

This hardly qualifies dancing as either a subversive activity or a measure of cultural disintegration. Before dancing can be condemned as a rebellious pastime, it should be compared with other responses to alienation exhibited down through the ages, including criminal activity, violence, cult membership, and even serious physical illness.

Compared with these manifestations of youthful alienation, dancing is surely the most benign, and ultimately, it may actually be beneficial to social and cultural development.

CHAPTER FIVE

The Glamour and the Business

BY ITS VERY NATURE THE ACT of dancing is exhibitionistic. The dancer seeks to become the object of attention either of his or her partner or of a team of steely-eyed judges on the perimeter of the ballroom floor.

In such an environment, style and attitude play almost as large a role as footwork and figures. It is not enough to move in precise time to the music, executing graceful steps and spins. Ballroom dancing is as much aura as action, firmly rooted in glamour and romance, and while it may be true that wonderful dancers can captivate an audience whatever their wardrobe, a proper costume improves everything—the visual effect, the dancers' confidence, and their freedom to move.

Ginger Rogers recognized the glamour potential when she commanded the wardrobe designer to create a special gown for her "Cheek to Cheek" number with Fred Astaire in the 1935 movie *Top Hat*. Rogers insisted on a blue dress (even though the film was in black and white). Not just "blue," but "pure blue

Subtlety is often no virtue, especially for Latin dancers. Everything is chosen to emphasize color, drama, and attitude.

with no green in it at all. Like the blue you find in the paintings of Monet."[1] She also directed that it be made of satin with many ostrich feathers, cut low in the back and high in the front.

She knew her stuff. The dress moved in rhythm with her body, adding grace to her steps and excitement to her spins. (It also added problems to Astaire's role when the ostrich feathers began to molt, causing him to sneeze frequently and demanding many retakes, but never mind....)

Next to the skill and precision of the dancers themselves, the most stunning first impression at a ballroom dance competition is the beauty of the gowns and accessories worn by the women.

Begin with the gowns worn for International Standard and American Smooth dances. For a few dark decades after World War II, ballroom gowns were short, hideous, pouffy creations worn over a dozen or more starched petticoats. Fortunately, Ginger Rogers's 1935 inspiration was revived during the 1980s. Hemlines were lowered, feathers grew popular again, boas and fringes were added, and ball gowns began to flow with the dancers.

Colors in today's ballroom dance gowns range from pale pastels to severe black-and-white, from shimmering gold or silver lamé to magnificent embroidered tapestry or light and lacy patterns. The attention of dance partners, audiences, and judges is drawn by bodice inserts of contrasting fabric and color, and heavy appliqués of sequins or rhinestones.

Hemlines hover between lower ankle and mid-calf, and a single garment may require fifteen or more yards of charmeuse, silk, or chiffon fabric. To add life to the fabrics, gown designers sew heavy fishline or bone inserts into dress hemlines, making them ripple and vibrate even when the wearer is standing still.

These are not fashions to be worn anywhere but in the spotlight of a ballroom competition. Nor are they selected as frivolously as an off-the-rack frock for a social event. Ballroom gowns represent a major investment, upwards of $5,000 each or more, and top competitors insist on at least two or three in their wardrobe. To ease their way into serious ballroom dancing, women might begin with a ready-to-wear or previously

American Smooth dancing style permits open dance positions and spins, so gowns are cut to rise during these steps. The result can be dramatic and sexy...or sometimes merely embarrassing.

The often haughty expression of male dancers in tails may have its roots in the basic discomfort of their garments: high-waisted trousers, stiff plastic collars, and jackets cut to emphasize a ramrod back and horizontal shoulders.

worn gown, available from a wide range of sources and suppliers, all of whom attend competitions to display their wares and accept orders.

COLOR, FABRIC, HEMLINE, and appliqués may be personal choices of the wearer, but her decision on other aspects of the gown will be based on the dancing style she and her partner will be performing.

International Standard styles—slow waltz, Viennese waltz, fox-trot, tango, and quick-step—require the partners to maintain a closed position, facing each other. As a result, the back of the woman's gown becomes more visible to observers than the front, even though the woman may display herself in waltzes and fox-trots by leaning well back from her partner in an over-sway. Thus, International Standard dancers tend to choose gowns with heavy boas and lots of "floats" on the arms and shoulders—anything to catch the judges' eyes and emphasize the coordinated moves of the dancers.

Couples dancing American Smooth, however, frequently break from the closed position in virtually every dance. Now both the front and back of the gown grow equally important, and many details chosen for International Standard gowns are no longer practical. Gowns worn in American Smooth competitions must look good in virtually any position, and items that may be useful when the dancer's arms are raised to meet her partner's in the closed position could tangle when the woman breaks and performs intricate moves not associated with Standard figures.

Spectacular spins in American Smooth dancing create their own demands and dangers. To encourage a rising hemline during spins, gowns worn by American Smooth performers are cut with more fullness and many are slit at least thigh-high. Fully cut gowns and fast spins do not always produce a graceful appearance, however. The gown that sweeps so graciously during a gliding waltz or fox-trot may resemble a tarpaulin in a wind storm when the dancer performs an overly enthusiastic spin.

Still, women who expect to perform in both International Standard and American Smooth will choose a dress suitable for American Smooth steps as a compromise.

Dancing International Latin or American Rhythm is quite another matter. Latin and jive/swing dancing is by nature more openly exuberant (but not necessarily more physically demanding) than Standard and Smooth steps. As a result, the costumes worn by women who perform these dances are skimpy and clinging. Spandex is a favorite fabric, although virtually any material

can be used effectively. Fringes and ruffles add motion, but essentially Latin dance costumes can be as imaginative and provocative as modesty and social standards permit.

MALE DANCERS LACK THE RANGE OF costume choices available to their female partners, especially in International Standard and American Smooth categories. For these performances, white tie and tails are de rigueur. Some men, especially in more liberal American Smooth competitions, stretch the dress code to accommodate fabrics in deep chocolate brown or with subtle pinstriping, but the basic items remain fixed and immutable: a tail suit with bow tie, white waistcoat, and stiff shirt with wing collar.

The jacket of a tail suit features a short cutaway front requiring a pair of high-waisted trousers and white waistcoat or vest extending over shirt and trouser top. The shirt itself is collarless, requiring a detachable plastic collar.

Showing up for almost anything except a dance competition or formal wedding in such a getup would be unheard of in the twenty-first century. But the tail suits worn by competitive ballroom dancers have no other practical use anyway, since they are sewn exclusively for ballroom dance use. Fabrics are tight-fitting nylon blends that resist bunching at the shoulders when the arms are elevated, and the entire garment is constructed with this one position in mind.

The arms for ballroom tails are attached quite differently from those on a jacket worn for social occasions. Armholes and sleeves are cut to produce a flat shoulder line when the arms are raised, and they feel uncomfortable in most other positions. Trousers button tightly just beneath the rib cage, giving an impression of extended leg length, and the starched shirts feature a hard white plastic collar. Elastics or other mechanical devices are often inserted to hold the jacket in place while dancing, and precisely measured weights may be added to the tail tips, enough to hold the tails vertically when standing still yet allow just the right amount of motion when dancing. The tails themselves may cross each other in the back when the man's

Male apparel for Latin dances can be as form-fitting as that for women, but black is favored as a contrasting foil to the bright colors of the ladies' costumes.

Dance footwear is highly sophisticated in design. Steel shanks add strength to the lightweight construction, and the soles employ a rough suede texture to add "feel" on the floor.

arms are lowered, so they will hang precisely vertical when his arms are raised for dancing.

Comfort is the last thing considered in the design and fit of a fine tail suit. All is sacrificed to generate a china-doll appearance for the man. Ballroom dancing is one of the few social pastimes—perhaps the only one—in which the female is costumed in greater comfort than the male.

Like the ball gowns worn by women in International Standard dancing, the backs of the men's costumes are the most visible, demanding special attention. The fit at the base of the neck is very important in stressing the man's posture and his upright bearing, and the amount of shirt collar showing above the jacket at the back may be measured with micrometer accuracy.

Most male International Standard or American Smooth dancers require only one set of tails. Except for rank beginners on a budget, who may purchase a used tail suit and alter it for their physique, tail suits are made-to-measure, most often in the United Kingdom. Average cost for jacket, trousers, and waistcoat will approach $1,500.

Ballroom dancing, even at the professional level, is not a high-income-generating activity. For many couples their wardrobe investment, on top of travel and accommodation expenses to attend major competitions, places tremendous strain on their financial resources. Yet dance they must, and always in the finest accoutrements available. Every dance competitor has stories to tell of ballroom dance couples who sweep across the floor with all the elegance of Prince Rainier and Princess Grace on their wedding night, only to retire when the evening is over to munch cold sandwiches and sleep in their car, avoiding the expense of a decent hotel room.

For Latin dances, men have more leeway in their wardrobe selection, but an unspoken rule limits them to costumes less spectacular than their female partner's. Here the message is the same, and only the gender changes. Male Latin dancers tend to choose shimmering shirts with wide collars and blousy sleeves, the top buttons left open to navel-nudging depth. Trousers, usually in black, tend to cling to the hips and buttocks.

GOWNS, TAIL SUITS, AND LATIN COSTUMES may catch the judges' eyes, but when it comes to a dancer's true comfort and top performance, nothing is more important than the shoes on their feet.

Footwear for competitive dancers is as specialized as any other item in their wardrobe. Flexibility in both the uppers and sole is key, of course, but so are strength and lightness. Ballroom dance shoes include a metal tang in the arch for extra support and a rough suedelike material on the soles. The sole material, referred to as "chrome leather" to reflect the specialized tanning process, would soon disintegrate if worn on concrete or in damp weather instead of indoors on a polished parquet floor. The rough suede surface provides a better "feel" of the floor surface than polished leather.

Most women who compete in Latin/Rhythm dances select shoes with T-straps, to prevent the shoe from becoming airborne during enthusiastic figures, plus round closed toes and heels about two and a half to three inches in height. Beginners might choose Cuban heels, an inch lower and wider at the base for better stability. For International Standard dancers, the preference is a plain satin pump dyed to match the gown.

Shoes for men are also specialized, permitting more flexibility in the soles and especially the uppers; normal dress shoes would soon crack and split from excessive use in a flexed position as the dancer rises and descends on tiptoes. Top-quality dance shoes for men and women cost about $100 per pair.

Some amateur Latin and jive dancers are attracted to athletic shoes for their routines. But the same shoes that aid Michael Jordan in performing a slam dunk are a serious barrier to Latin and jive dancers during their spins and turns. Athletic shoes grip the floor too aggressively, and some dancers have suffered serious knee injuries when the torsion power exerted during a dance maneuver was simply too high for their knee joint to handle.

The comfort of shoes by Nike, Reebok, and others can't be ignored, however, nor can their suitability as part of a contemporary dancer's costume. In an effort to obtain the best of both worlds, some dancers apply chrome leather to the soles. Others

One description of accessories for female dancers is "Las Vegas Excess." Beads, necklaces, earrings, and hairstyles are all selected to catch the eyes of judges across a crowded floor.

have found a cheaper solution with bowling shoes, whose flexible uppers and chrome leather soles match the needs of a dance floor precisely, but at a third of the cost.

WOMEN ENHANCE THEIR ON-FLOOR impact with accessories ranging from hairstyles and jewelry to methods of embellishing aspects of their body that, in their opinion, nature may have failed to fulfill.

Costume jewelry sparkling amid the spotlights draws a judge's attention during a dance. But the impact of necklaces and pendants is severely limited when the woman dances in the closed position, facing her partner. Thus, International Standard dancers devote more attention to other items, especially earrings.

Austrian crystal earrings are especially favored, although not for pierced ears. Even during relatively sedate waltzes and quicksteps, accidents may occur, producing bloody and painful results for wearers of oversized pierced-ear accessories. Clip-on earrings can't be trusted to stay put during active dancing, so dancers explore other solutions to secure their earrings, including super glue and Velcro. A safer solution is small squares of two-sided foam-core carpet tape attached to both surfaces of an earring clip and pressed securely against the earlobe.

Even more critical than jewelry is a woman dancer's hairstyle, and this presents its own challenges. Makeup, nails, and accessories can all be prepared and perfected at or near the dance venue, but no one can expect to find hairdressers on the fringe of the ballroom dance floor. In fact, few hairdressers are qualified to create the often excessive styles suitable for ballroom performances. This is especially important for International Standard and American Smooth dancers, whose hair is expected to be long, feminine, and dramatically styled, yet firmly fixed to prevent it from shielding the dancer's face during exuberant spins. To add to the problem, some dance competitions extend over two days or more. Do some women dancers sleep sitting up to preserve their hairstyles from day to day? Possibly. More likely, however, they exchange ingenious solutions with each other, such as sleeping with their hair wrapped in a satin pillowcase.

Latin dancers have things easier—at least where hairstyles are concerned. Short hair on women Latin dancers is chic and more than acceptable, as are ponytails.

Male dancers in International Standard and American Smooth competitions require a short, conservative haircut with a clean line along the back of the neck. Mustaches are barely acceptable, and beards are as rare as button-down collars.

In Latin dances virtually anything goes for men, including ponytails, shoulder-length tresses, and any facial hair the man chooses to cultivate.

When skill, athleticism, and presentation come together during the dance, the result pleases crowds, impresses judges, and wins awards.

BALLROOM DANCE COMPETITIONS ARE MORE than an event to determine winners in each category. They are also business opportunities for companies that supply the dancers with products ranging from gowns and tail suits to shoes, makeup, accessories, and special energy-boosting foods.

None of the wardrobe suppliers dedicated to ballroom and DanceSport activities will ever rival Ralph Lauren or Burberry for size, wealth, or influence. But they remain aggressive designers and marketers nevertheless, renting as much total exhibit space during the Blackpool Festival as the entire four-thousand-square-foot dance floor. Between practice sessions and events, dancers roam through the exhibits, selecting gowns, fabrics, shoes, accessories, and other items such as foam inserts capable of boosting bust measurements sufficiently to produce Edwardian-era hourglass figures. Other booths hawk canned formulations for dancers to gulp before setting out on the floor, strange concoctions whose primary ingredients appear to be fruit juice, caffeine, and vitamin supplements; and self-tanning lotions that enable the couple to appear as though they stepped directly onto the dance floor from a month in Jamaica.

Among the most aggressive promoters of ballroom-based products are companies specializing in dance music on CDs, and dance performances and lessons on videotape.

The music is an essential element for beginning dancers and serious dance competitors, since it is rarely found on contemporary mainstream labels. Tracks are identified by the name of the dance to be performed and include the beats-per-minute of the music, played by orchestras well known among many ballroom fans. Except at the championship level, very little of the dance music includes vocals. Dancers, with the exception of those selecting soul music, prefer to concentrate on steady rhythm and sweeping melodies, avoiding the intrusion of lyrics, story lines, and piercing voices.

Producers of videotapes are just as prominent as CD marketers at dance events, although video purchasers are likely more passive in their use of this medium. Only the basic dance steps can be communicated by videotape, after all, and one suspects

that most tape buyers choose the video productions either to learn new, more dramatic presentation techniques or as a record of classic dance performances by exceptional dancers in a superlative setting.

Finally, another business aspect of dancing is provided by video production houses that contract with individual dancers to record their competitive performances on tape. At most dance festivals, especially in the United States, a bank of camcorders is positioned to cover the dance floor with a dozen or more tripod-mounted units, each panning and zooming to follow an individual couple through their steps and figures. Later, in the comfort of their living rooms or the confines of their dance studio, the partners can dissect their movements frame by frame, spotting elements here and there to refine and improve upon, moving up the competition ladder rung by rung.

NONE OF THIS, WITH THE EXCEPTION of footwear perhaps, affects the actual dance steps performed by the partners. Yet all of it contributes to attitude and confidence, twin pillars of success for any aspiring dance pair.

Any sign of indecision or ambiguity by dancing partners is fatal to their opportunity of not only winning a competition but executing their steps and figures correctly. Almost as destructive can be ignorance or rejection of the required facial expression to be worn during each dance. For International Standard and American Smooth dancers, this means giddy delight from the woman in virtually every dance except the tango and, for the man, a choice between either smug self-confidence or haughty arrogance. Latin dancers, performing all but the paso doble, are expected to display either the public passion of two people in love or a limitless childlike joy and exuberance at the pure pleasure of each other's company.

From time to time a couple steps onto the dance floor prepared to execute all the steps and figures precisely as directed in the various syllabus guidelines, but without the joy and intensity demanded by the dance. Their moves may be impeccable, their floorcraft precise, and their rhythm as tightly cued to the music as a symphonic conductor's. But when their countenance is wrong—when the woman frowns through her moves and the man exhibits concern over his footwork—the exercise fails and both we and the couple are doomed to disappointment.

For all the magic to be communicated, dancing must be both sternly practiced and unconsciously performed. We want to believe that the dancers are living out a portion of their lives on the parquet, opening corners of their souls to us as they dance—otherwise, what else can the dance express?

If this makes actors of the finest dancers, so be it. The same motivation, the same expectation of a public enamored of romance, has made dancers out of some of the finest actors, after all.

CHAPTER SIX

The Dancing Life

THE IMPULSE TO DANCE, TO EMPLOY the human body as a tool of kinetic expression, is so powerful that it inspires parody in comic strips and Broadway productions. The image of Gene Kelly, wearing a plaid jacket and shouting "Gotta dance!" over and over again like a mantra, strengthened the perception of competitive ballroom dancers as compulsive individuals anxious to pay the price of sprained ankles, strained muscles, and social indifference in return for a few moments of glory on the dance floor.

Like all clichés, there is an element of truth rooted in this conception. But as with all stereotypes, the preconceptions begin to break down when applied not to groups but to individuals.

MARCUS AND KAREN HILTON are everything we expect from a couple who, wherever they step onto a dance floor to practice their craft, walk away with the glory and silverware as undisputed champions.

They have been doing this almost from their teenage years, when they formed a dancing partnership that blossomed first

Robert Tang and Beverley Cayton-Tang sacrifice leisure time and incur substantial expense in pursuit of dance competitions throughout North America and Europe. Their many rewards include the title of North American Amateur Standard Dance Champions.

into marriage and then into one of the most dominating teams in the history of competitive dance. Marcus, who began dancing at age eight, was representing the United Kingdom in international events just six years later. At age fifteen, he and his then-partner won the British Junior Latin American Championship at Blackpool. Two years later he teamed with a new partner named Karen Johnstone.

Karen began her competitive dancing career soon after taking her first ballroom dance lessons at age seven (she had been dancing ballet for four years). In 1978 she was teamed with Marcus Hilton, already a rising star. At that moment, each found their partner in dancing and in life.

Just eighteen and seventeen years of age respectively, Marcus and Karen soon attracted so much attention for their natural grace and obvious talents that their local town council awarded a grant to assist them in financing their training and travel. Even their local member of Parliament, Sir Cyril Smith, offered his support.

For several years, the couple supported their passion for dance by working at regular jobs such as truck driver and warehouse packer. The jobs provided both a reasonable income and the opportunity to travel in pursuit of dancing championships.

Travel they did, representing Britain as amateurs in both Latin and Ten-Dance championships (performing both five Standard and five Latin dances) at competitions throughout Europe and as far afield as Hong Kong. After a steady climb up the ladder, they won the World and European Ten-Dance championships in 1981, received the Carl Alan Award for Outstanding Amateur Couple in 1982, turned professional in 1983, and married in 1986.

By their mid-thirties the Hiltons had won the British Open and European championships five times each, and the World Championship seven times. These have been International Standard competitions, where the elegance of the Hiltons has simply dominated the field.

Impressive enough. But Marcus and Karen have achieved success in fields considered far beyond the reach of ordinary mortals.

In the world of competitive dancing, Marcus and Karen Hilton have achieved virtually royal status—a distinction underlined when they were named Members of the British Empire by Queen Elizabeth.

They achieved World Amateur Championship status in Latin dances before turning professional, and in 1986 won the World Ten-Dance Championship as professionals—a feat involving all five International Standard dances plus all five International Latin steps, the dance equivalent of the Olympic decathlon.

It may be demanding at the top, but in the Hiltons' case it does not appear to be lonely. Virtually everyone expresses affection for the couple, the words of praise untainted by the jealousies or petty assessments associated with many other competitive pastimes.

They adhere to a rigorous training schedule between dance events, practicing two to three hours daily and doubling this amount of time in preparation for major competitions. In addition, they give dance lessons to hordes of students who are eager to touch the hems of the champions. Their intensely competitive nature is belied by their elegant, almost patrician bearing on the dance floor and their casual accessibility when chatting with admirers off it.

But when the costumes are on and the music begins, the Hiltons become quietly elegant tigers, as determined to sweep away upstart challengers as any top-level competitors on a football field, baseball diamond, or hockey rink.

"We have been champions for so long that everybody is there to beat us," Marcus Hilton has observed. "We treat every competition like a battle, and every one is different. So we work out a game plan for each one and size up the floor, the audience, the music."

Their long reign at the top of International Standard dancing is due as much to their work ethic as to their talents and skill. After all these years they still refuse to take their dominance for granted, and the couple are constantly working to remove even the smallest fault or perceived weakness in their dancing.

Surprising as it may be to some, the Hiltons modify their choreography to suit the dance competition venue. This goes beyond adjusting their routines to suit the shape and dimensions of certain ballroom floors. Dancing in a converted sports hall with bright lighting and tiered seating is quite a different matter to the Hiltons from performing at Blackpool, with three levels of stalls and dramatic arc lights sweeping constantly across the floor.

Preparation for a major dance event involves six hours of

practice each day in their London studio, plus dance lessons they give to students.

Marcus Hilton believes that physical fitness alone cannot pave the way to dance success. "I feel dancing is an artistic sport," he once pointed out. "We need to be fit to do what we do, but it is not just about fitness. You have to be artistic in the presentation, timing, and musicality. We warm up and warm down a lot, but we are also careful not to build up muscles in the wrong places, or add extra pounds of flesh."

Looking back over their career, what would they be doing if they were not dancing? Marcus and Karen glance at each other and smile. "I think we would be testing cars," Marcus suggests.

Karen nods agreement. "Fast cars," she adds.

Their automobiles reflect that ambition, so far removed from the demands of the ballroom dance floor. It also suggests that, at the level of success reached by the Hiltons, dancing's rewards extend beyond the dance studio and the awards table: Marcus drives a Lexus and Karen drives across the English countryside in a Lotus.

NO SUCH PERKS ARE ENJOYED by Robert Tang and Beverley Cayton-Tang, although they take every bit as much pride in their room full of dance trophies as the Hiltons would in a garage full of luxury cars. North American Amateur Standard Dance champions for two consecutive years, Robert and Beverley have earned wide acclaim and the respect of their competitors.

From their condominium home west of Toronto, Beverley commutes daily to her work as a supervisor for local libraries while Robert works in the computer software marketing industry. The traditional concept of a relaxing holiday is unknown to the Tangs. Every hour of paid vacation time or leave of absence is devoted to attending dance competitions or participating in dance demonstrations and media events.

Like many successful dance teams, Robert and Beverley are the product of natural inherent skill, dedicated training and practice, and the critical yet unpredictable effects of two personalities thinking as one. Unlike others, however, their partnership began rather late and their ascendance to championship level has been spectacular; they won their first major competition within six months of forming their dancing partnership.

Beverley began her dance training at age eight in her native England by accompanying her older brother to dance class. But it wasn't the thrill of gliding across the floor in perfect step with her partner that first intrigued her.

"It was the dresses!" she laughs. "As a little girl, sitting on the edge of the ballroom floor and watching all the couples dance past, I was mesmerized by the beautiful gowns the ladies wore. They would swish past my face with all the sound of silk and satin and chiffon. I just wanted to wear one of those dresses, and if I had to learn to dance first, that was fine with me!"

Beverley achieved more than a glamorous ball gown. She blossomed during her dance lessons, earning bronze and silver status by age eleven, when she immigrated to Canada with her parents.

"Dancing in Canada hadn't reached the heights it enjoyed in England," she recalls, "and it was difficult to find a good dance school." But find one she did, and as time passed she enjoyed it more and more. Performing both Standard and Latin, she eventually teamed up with a partner and rose to third-place amateur ranking in Canada for Standard dances.

Robert, born in Malaysia, also immigrated to Canada as a child. Also, like Beverley, his parents had been dance enthusiasts and he saw dance lessons as another challenge, another barrier to be surmounted by the child of immigrants in a racially different country.

"I thought dancing was a lark," he says with Beverley at his side, "mostly because the teachers made it fun. They encouraged me to learn and compete, and within three weeks of my first lesson they enrolled me in my first competition."

Robert's teachers noticed his ability to dance the fox-trot with a natural rise-and-fall, a graceful motion like the steady swell of the sea. Many dancers—especially men—may practice for years without mastering this essential motion, yet Robert

Many dance partners are married, and the arrival of children rarely interrupts their careers, although it can create new sideline distractions at competitions.

seemed to perform it virtually from the beginning with no training or practice.

Eventually Robert and Beverley were competing against each other, with their selected partners. As with virtually all dancers, the competition was friendly and good-natured, with each couple congratulating the other at every achievement.

But when Beverley's partner decided he wanted to pursue a professional career in dancing, she faced a crisis. "I wasn't prepared to become a professional," she points out. "I didn't really want to teach, and I felt there was so much more for me to learn."

Robert, meanwhile, was achieving great success in his lessons, although something was missing, something that prevented both him and his partner from breaking through to full championship status. Call it chemistry.

Encouraged by their dancing teacher, both teams sat down one day to discuss the situation. The solution was logical and predictable; it was the outcome that proved almost prophetic.

The two teams essentially changed partners. Robert's partner was intrigued by the idea of a professional career, which made her an ideal match for Beverley's partner. Robert had his own reasons for wanting to dance with Beverley.

"To tell you the truth," he grins shyly, "I had a crush on her."

The teenage vernacular quickly changes when Robert describes his first dance with Beverley—a description that resonates with other competitive dancers when they first encounter a new, symbiotic dancing relationship.

"She was like a Thoroughbred horse!" Robert says, and now it's Beverley's turn to blush. "Stepping on the floor and beginning to dance, I felt a surge of power from her. It was the most amazing thing!"

Something was happening here, and the resulting chemistry generated new incentive to refine their skills and meld them into a team whose sum accomplishments are far more than the individual partners might ever hope to achieve.

"We really began putting effort into our practice sessions," Robert recalls. "And the chemistry started to get even stronger. When we were on the floor, there was no sense that we were sharing anything beyond the dance. That's when it began taking over our lives."

"It was meant to be," Beverley says simply. "Everything about us, everything between us personally, we seemed able to transmit to the floor."

They grew united by more than dancing. In 1993, Robert

and Beverley became husband and wife (as did, it should be mentioned, their two former partners).

In performance, the Tangs project elegance and flair in every step, but they especially shine in the quick-step. "He flies!" Beverley says, almost in wonder at her husband/partner's proficiency. "There's a level of excitement to the quick-step that just seems to propel us past anything and anybody!"

Robert has an explanation. "The quick-step is the last of the five dances you perform in a Standard repertoire," he explains. "So it's your chance to atone for something you might have done, or failed to do, in any of the previous dances. Also, it's your chance to show off all the energy you have, leaving the others behind. You can make a statement about your enthusiasm and strength, and if the music is right, it sets the pace."

Their weakest dance? No hesitation here.

"It's the tango," Robert replies, and Beverley nods her head in agreement. "We're seeing more of the Argentine style of dancing, with lots of flicks and kicks. The Italians are especially good at the tango. They seem to have a special way of shifting their bodies that nobody else can quite match."

Bright, dedicated, and resourceful, the Tangs have gained almost as much fame in recent years for their promotion work on behalf of ballroom dancing and DanceSport as for their triumphs in competition. Robert designed and manages Dancescape, a major Internet site covering competition schedules, dancing news, personals, and other dance-related links. Dancescape may well pave the way for the Tangs' new career choice. Still not enamored of the idea of becoming dancing professionals, they plan to turn their talent toward organizing and promoting competitive dance events in the future.

"We have some ideas on how competitions should be run," Robert notes.

Which is hardly surprising, since they have proven on many occasions that they have many ideas on how competitions can be *won*.

RIPPLES OF EXCITEMENT ALWAYS sweep across a room when a professional rhythm dance event begins. But when Bob Powers and Julia Gorchakova take the floor, the ripples rise to tidal-wave expectations. Powers and Gorchakova seem to possess a reservoir of energy beyond human capability, and their dancing is never less than electric and rarely less than dominating.

Immediately following a performance, Bob Powers appears to have stepped out of a shower rather than off a dance floor. He is drenched in perspiration and still vibrating with excitement. Not blessed with the classic dancer's tall, thin physique, Powers instead draws upon a sense of dedication and limitless energy that suggests, in the midst of competition, nothing less than a miniature continuous nuclear explosion.

Curiously enough, in addition to overcoming the challenge of dancing with a body that looks more suited for the football field than for the ballroom, Powers didn't even begin to dance until late adolescence—practically middle age for some professional competitors. And it all began with a movie.

"I saw *Saturday Night Fever* when I was seventeen years old," Powers recalls, "and it changed me completely." The sight of John Travolta strutting across the screen in his white three-piece suit galvanized the Philadelphia native. He couldn't erase the vision from his mind. Dances performed in the movie were more than high-school shimmy dances. In *Saturday Night Fever* the men and women dance as couples, they follow routines and figures, they wear suits and dresses instead of jeans and T-shirts, and they dance in both open and closed positions. This wasn't the boring heel-and-toe steps performed in the high-school gymnasium; this was something Powers had never seen before, something he had never dreamed of.

Bob Powers walked into the movie theater as a curious teenager with no clear ambitions. He stepped out determined to become a dancer.

And he did. With impressive success. So impressive, in fact, that little more than a decade later he and a dancing partner were performing in Russia on a tour that included the historic city of St. Petersburg. Powers had achieved his goal of

The movie *Saturday Night Fever* and a dance tour of Russia combined to produce perhaps the world's most exciting Professional Latin dance team: Bob Powers and Julia Gorchakova.

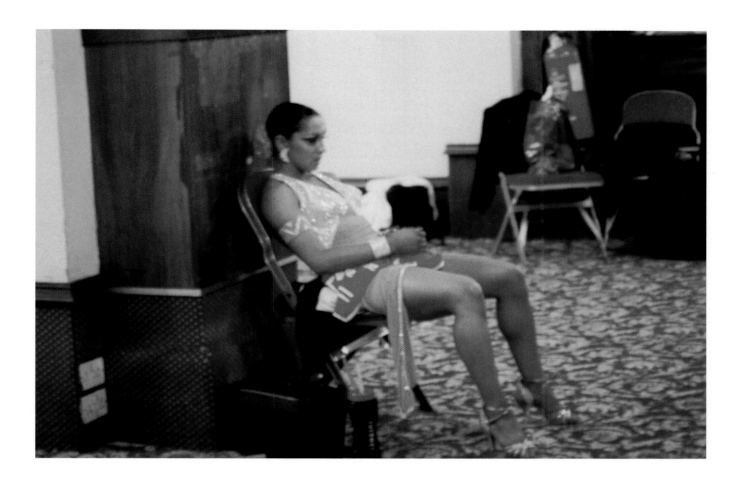

becoming a successful dancer, but something still eluded him. He and his partner performed well together. But a dancing couple is like a two-link length of chain, which means the weakest link determines its strength.

In St. Petersburg, Bob Powers discovered his new link.

Julia Gorchakova had begun dancing at a very early age, as many Russian youngsters do in the country that virtually invented ballet. Adding ballroom and Latin dancing to her skills, she performed as a teenager during one of Bob Powers's appearances in Russia, and Powers saw something in her dancing that ignited the fire still burning within him.

"I had gone as far as I could go with my current partner," Powers recalls. "But when I saw Julia dance, I just knew we could do great things together. I just *knew*."

Powers was so entranced by Julia's skill, and so convinced of their special symbiosis, that he asked if she would dance with him—in secret. For the next few days, Bob and Julia danced

On the dance floor, all is glamour and excitement. But backstage or on the sidelines, awaiting the judges' decision and the next dance event, the mood is pensive and concerned; in some cases, total exhaustion takes over.

together out of sight and sound of everyone else. The chemistry was instant and astonishing, and when Bob's troupe returned home, he stayed behind with Julia.

When Julia immigrated to the United States in 1991, a new American Rhythm Championship team was launched. And when Bob and Julia married in 1994, they had reached the top echelon of Latin/Rhythm dancing.

Success comes with a price to pay. Both partners run over four miles and practice a minimum of three hours each day. They frequently coach on behalf of Arthur Murray Studios and travel to major competitive events throughout the United States, leaving them little time to spend at their Scottsdale, Arizona, home.

But what about the other expected cost—the one to their marriage? Doesn't constant travel, practice, and competitive pressure place a strain on a relationship?

Julia agrees that it can. "We're best friends as well as dancing partners," she explains. "And that helps. If we have a bad practice at the studio, we just don't take it home with us."

And how about that energy? Where does it come from, and how do they keep it focused?

"I draw inspiration from the music," Bob says. "It drives me and keeps me going."

For Julia, the source is more internal. "I love to perform," she responds. "I love to work hard and make people applaud me. And when we're on the floor dancing, we feed off each other. When Bob does something amazing, I want to answer him with something amazing of my own."

"That's when we get the effect our coach calls 'that *thing*,'" Bob Powers notes. "That's when we know we're focused, when we're giving more than a hundred percent. Our coach says, 'Now you've got that *thing*!'" and he laughs at their mentor's limited attempt to describe the indescribable.

But everyone who sees Powers and Gorchakova dance knows precisely what it is.

THREE COUPLES FROM WIDELY differing backgrounds, the Hiltons, the Tangs, and Powers and Gorchakova all exhibit near-identical qualities off the dance floor: they are low-key, wholly approachable, and totally bereft of pretense or conceit.

Most competitive dancers reflect the same personality, the same rejection of prima donna attitudes, perhaps because dancing fulfills any need for identity and banishes any serious questions about self-worth.

"Dancing," one competitor explained, "gives me an opportunity to express things on the dance floor I wouldn't dare reveal anywhere else. I can become a different person, a show-off, an exhibitionist even. But I'm not that way in the rest of my life. It's a strange thing that happens when I dance, and I'm not sure I'll ever understand it.

"But I'm not sure that I could live without it now, either...."

CHAPTER SEVEN

Romancing the Judge

BALLROOM DANCERS AND JUDGES alike face the same conundrum faced by everyone associated with competitions based on expression and originality: How does one make accurate comparative judgments?

All adjudicators, from baseball umpires to Academy Award voters, are subject to assessment and condemnation by both participants and spectators. In some sports, the opportunity to second-guess and loudly criticize referees and umpires is a major attraction to fans.

It is a tribute to the participants in DanceSport that judges are rarely, if ever, openly criticized by dancers or spectators. Some speculate that dancers may refrain from candidly criticizing a judge, fearing vengeful wrath in a future competition. Yet, more than a few competitive ice skaters have severely berated judges, and spectators at skating events often boo and hiss without restraint at a score they consider unfair and unfavorable to the skater.

When dance audiences disagree with the decision of the judging panel, their tactics are quite different, yet probably more effective. At one major international dance festival, the audience

Everything is perfection, including posture, expression, motion, and visual impact. But the judges, visible in the background, are looking in another direction.

was clearly in favor of a particular professional Latin couple. When the favored couple placed only third, they received a standing ovation from the crowd, who in contrast clearly restrained themselves at the announcement of the first-place winners. No boos, no hisses, no shouts of reproach were heard. Instead, the audience reversed the usual response, choosing to praise their favorite instead of berating either judges or winners.

There is some question whether this sense of reserve and fair play will continue when DanceSport grows more intense under the glare of extended television coverage, powered by major sponsorship and substantial prizes. Television producers in the United States already delight in encouraging the audience and competitors to chant nationalist slogans ("*USA! USA!*") during team competitions.

Perhaps the elegance and romance of the dance, and the valued camaraderie of the dancers themselves, will shield the sport from some of the darker aspects of intense competition for substantial awards and wide recognition.

Dance judges, positioned on the perimeter of the dance area, face the challenge of selecting the best half-dozen competitors among those on an often crowded floor.

THE ROLE OF DANCE JUDGES is not made any easier by the extensive range of dance categories and syllabi. Within the United States, dance competitions may or may not be based upon American Smooth and American Rhythm dances. They may, for example, include separate categories for the merengue, bolero, East Coast and West Coast swing, and other unique steps.

Things grow even more complex with the multiple levels of awards for each dance category: Rising Stars, Bronze, Silver, and Gold. At the bronze, silver, and gold levels, most U.S. dance teachers and studios agree that each level at least suggests the following stages of dance development:

Bronze	Patterns and techniques associated with basic social ballroom dancing
Silver	Patterns and techniques associated with advanced ballroom dancing
Gold	Competitive level: performance-oriented and highly technical

The difficulty arises when trying to assign a single set of figures for any given medal range. One U.S. dance authority has identified eleven different "official" syllabi!

On the international scene, dance competitions tend to be more tightly structured, and at Blackpool, the concentration is entirely on championship-caliber performances. Even so, the various categories may leave the newcomer confused. Here is a typical list, as they appeared in chronological order, of dance events held over nine consecutive days at Blackpool:

Rising Stars Latin
Senior Modern
Under 21 Years Latin
Amateur Latin
Rising Stars Modern
Senior Latin
Under 21 Years Modern
Amateur Modern
Professional Latin
Professional Modern

Judges rank couples according to the dance being performed. Thus, partners may be rated first in some dances and last in others by the same judge, although this rarely occurs.

Most of the dances extend over two days, with preliminary heats starting one morning and the finals not taking place until late in the evening of the following day.

This is a long, complex, and enervating process. As many as sixteen heats may be required, with up to twenty-four couples per heat, before moving to the next level of twelve heats. From there the field is narrowed through four rounds to the semi-finals, where twelve outstanding couples compete for the final six positions; from these final six emerge the winners and ranked runners-up.

As a result, a competing Latin couple may perform eight times over two days, each performance requiring them to execute five individual dances as close to perfection as their bodies, skill, and determination permit.

While the challenge may be daunting for the dancers, it is no less so for the judges. Positioned at various locations around the

perimeter of the dance floor, pencil and score sheet in hand, each judge has little more than two minutes to scan as many as twenty-four couples constantly moving through his or her line of sight.

Fortunately, the actual scoring process is simplified as much as possible. Each judge "calls back" a fixed number of couples by individual dance, identifying them by numbers worn on the man's back. Usually the number of dance couples to be rated (or "called back") in each heat is six, but in large competitions it could be double.

In the final round, each judge places all the competing couples in order of merit for each dance, rating the best couple for that dance as one, the next as two, and so on. Ties are not permitted. The winner of a particular dance is the couple who were placed first by an absolute majority of judges.

Should a tie for absolute majority occur, the adjudicators move down to see which of the tied couples had an absolute majority for second place, assigning them first place. The same rule applies for other placements as well.

One dancing couple may be rated in second place for the waltz, fifth for the tango, first for the quick-step, and so on. In reality, however, the placings are usually much closer than this, and it is highly unusual for a couple to be placed first in one dance figure and last in another by the same judge during the same sequence.

IN COMPETITION, DANCERS ARE EXPECTED to adequately perform a number of basic moves and steps according to their competitive level—bronze, silver, or gold. To the beginner, the steps and figures are bewildering in their number, complexity, and arcane description.

Consider this syllabus from the International Dance Teachers Association (IDTA) for the fox-trot. If you believe the fox-trot is an elemental walking-style dance, this may change your view of it forever. All competitive dancers must be prepared to demonstrate their mastery of these steps, level by level:

Bronze

    Basic Weave

    Change of Direction

    Closed Impetus

    Feather Step

    Natural Turn

    Reverse Turn and Feather Finish

    Reverse Wave

    Three-step

Silver

    Closed Telemark

    Hover Feather

    Hover Telemark

    Natural Telemark

    Natural Twist Turn

    Natural Weave

    Open Impetus

    Open Telemark with Feather Ending

    Open Telemark, Natural Turn, Outside Swivel,
       Feather Ending

    Quick Natural Weave

    Quick Open Reverse

    Reverse Pivot

    Top Spin

    Weave from PP

Gold

    Back Feather

    Bounce Fallaway with Weave Ending

    Curved Feather

    Curved Three-step

    Extended Reverse Wave

    Fallaway Reverse, Slip Pivot

    Hover Cross

    Natural Hover Telemark

    Natural Zig-Zag from PP

Technique and presentation are key qualities assessed by dance judges. But these are often supplemented by less easily articulated measures, including the emotional impact generated by the dance partners.

Each of these steps is easily recognized by students of dance after sufficient lessons with a qualified teacher. In competition, the moves come instinctively or via extensive practice, and qualified judges recognize them without hesitation. Their presence is expected and unmarked; their absence is apparent and grounds for disqualification.

DANCE JUDGES ARE SELECTED from a wide roster of former dance champions, most of them now teaching and coaching. Those in the upper level of judging ability lead a peripatetic life, flying off to as many as a dozen events annually in Italy, Japan, Australia, and New Zealand as well as cities and small towns in North America and Europe.

Their expertise varies according to their experience and interest. Some restrict themselves to Latin/Rhythm dances or Standard/Smooth. Others are prepared to assess all ten International dances plus specialized steps such as West Coast swing and bolero. All, however, agree that much of dance judging is an opinion based on the judges' training, experience, and emotional response.

Dancers at the beginning or novice level can expect judges to focus on fundamentals and technique. But at upper levels of competition, the judges expect that technical aspects of the dance are well in hand. Here they begin to focus on the impression generated by the dancers' moves—their expression, their interpretation of the dance and its origins, and their musicality. Superb technique alone will not succeed at this level. The personalities of the dancers must shine through in the performance. As one highly regarded judge put it, "They have to make me feel good—about them, and about their performance."

Given that judges have barely ninety seconds to make their selection, it is little wonder that instinct and personal impression play such a vital role in the assessment process. Yet, tempered by experience, judges usually agree that many critical decisions are made quickly. Each judge has his or her own technique—usually a form of triage—to ease the decision making, and by the time the final six couples are performing, the

Away from the dance floor, partners may practice their steps in silence or, after a poorly assessed performance, commiserate in privacy.

ranking is a matter of divide and assess. Within the first thirty seconds, a judge can quickly divide the couples into the top three and bottom three. Then it's a matter of selecting the best among the top three and the most wanting among the bottom three. Often the most difficult decision is not among those who place first and last but the third and fourth positions, where one impulsive, exhilarating step may elevate the couple a level or two, and one misstep or grimace may slip them down a notch.

Such subjective assessment leads, from time to time, to puzzling outcomes at even the most prestigious competitions. More than once, five judges have selected a couple first in all dances, while the sixth judge placed the same couple in last place for every dance.

It may be maddening to dancers and spectators, but dancing is first and foremost an expression of individual emotion, and there can be little surprise when judges respond in the same manner.

DANCERS SEEK EVERY ADVANTAGE possible to add to their confidence and visibility during a dance performance, and their effort extends far beyond wardrobe, makeup, and accessories. Competitive dancers note the precise location of each judge around the dance floor, and many will virtually challenge a judge to ignore their presence and performance. Saving their best figures until they arrive in front of a judge, they posture, preen, and virtually seduce (in the broadest terms) the judge with smiles, gestures, and expressions.

It is the judge's duty, of course, to remain unmoved by such entreaties, although more than one judge has had to physically step backward to prevent a collision with an overly enthusiastic couple who insisted on sweeping so close they appear to be inviting the judge to share the next figure with them.

Nor is the prospect of a collision with a judge the only concern. In some corners, rumblings are being heard about the rising incidence of "dirty dancing."

The phrase has nothing to do with a disapproving parent's

description of teenage rock 'n' roll dance routines. After all, the most outrageous steps practiced on a dance floor in the 1950s would fail to raise an eyebrow at a first-rate Latin dance competition today. "Dirty dancing" refers to the risk of injury from reckless or dangerously aggressive practices during top-level dance competitions.

Rising competition raises new barriers to be breached and new limits to be tested if victory is to be achieved. That is why, year after year, the waltz, fox-trot, and quick-step are performed at faster foot speed, incorporating more pivots, leaps, and spins than before.

Similar developments have occurred in competitive ice skating, where today's top performers are expected to include triple and even quadruple turns when vying for victory, elements unheard of a generation ago. The difference, of course, is that skaters have the entire ice surface to themselves during their performance. In DanceSport, couples share the same ballroom space with a dozen or more other competitors, all equally determined to impress the judges and elevate their final standings.

Even masters of floorcraft are unable to avoid serious collisions from time to time, especially if the other couple involved are paying insufficient attention to their speed and direction. The results can be painful and severe. One top amateur Latin dancer suffered major injury to her knee when kicked by the overenthusiastic couple next to her. It took several months for the victim to recover and compete again. Another woman, her hand held in fixed position for the opening of a paso doble, had her thumb broken by a sudden sweep of an adjoining couple's hand at the beginning of the music. Ignoring the intense pain, she managed to finish both the paso doble and jive before collapsing in agony.

But these are accidents. More distressing has been a perceived rise in intentional collisions, to the point where couples are quite literally knocked off their feet. While these remain rare and often unsubstantiated events, regulators of the sport claim a strict code of conduct is necessary, especially when the stakes are raised through wider media coverage and Olympic recognition.

Among the key skills of successful dancers is floorcraft: the ability to avoid collisions with other dancers while appearing unaware of their presence.

Some rules are already in place. A dancer who loses a shoe must stop immediately and replace the shoe before continuing, to prevent injury to other couples.

Declaring that all competitors must move around the floor in a counterclockwise rotation is a basic rule, one often difficult to enforce when up to twenty-four intensely competitive couples are vying for the judges' attention.

A large contingent of dancing enthusiasts regret the need for major modifications to an elegant pastime. Introduction of a strict disciplinary code and major modifications to the ballroom itself, they argue, would transform ballroom dancing from a genteel courting ritual to a fiercely competitive vocation in search of fame and fortune.

Interestingly, most concerns about "dirty dancing" emanate from Britain. One observer noted that dancing "is the last sport in which Britain still leads the world in expertise, tuition and prize money." But in the next sentence the writer darkly adds: "Competitors from all over the world have brought the manners of the football stadium and boxing ring to the dance floor."[1]

THE RANKING PROCESS during dance competitions remains in some ways more deeply rooted in the judges' impressions of each couple's performance than in their execution of steps and figures as prescribed by whatever syllabus governs the competition. In other words, the subjective impression of the dance performance carries more weight than an objective assessment.

Here are actual criticisms from a judge and dance writer, prepared for a dance publication in reviewing a major U.S. event in 1996:[2]

"Their sides looked flat, and feet need attention."

"Nancy's back was dropped and it seemed as if David's weight wasn't very well centered."

"The next step will be to soften her back and leg actions, and for the entire frame to be contained better."

"I found their leg actions hard, feet not used to the

fullest extent, and shaping over-produced from the top."

"I'd like to see Tammy a little more poised with a positive posture. This will allow her to use her back more effectively and help keep the weight more forward on her feet."

"I'd like to see Robert correct his upper back posture. To bring it a little more forward will stop him counter-balancing his own swing and will help further the development of superior movement and body flight."

This is superb constructive criticism, perhaps unmatched in its honesty and value by any similar competitive event.

In reality, however, judges need no such rationalization for the marks they assign each couple. It is necessary only to rank them according to the dance performed. In another admirable aspect of competitive dancing, all rankings are posted for the dancers to review, enabling them to identify the strength and weakness in their performance as determined by individual judges.

CHAPTER EIGHT

All the World's a Dance Floor

IF THE BLACKPOOL DANCE FESTIVAL did not exist, no one would think of inventing it.

After all, who could seriously propose conducting the world's most prestigious ballroom dancing event in a seaside resort so removed from the salons and studios of London and New York?

Reportedly, Blackpool has as many hotel rooms as all of Portugal, the vast majority in small family-operated establishments geared to working-class vacationers. The town's most attractive feature is a wide sandy beach fronting the Irish Sea that serves as a backdrop for a continuous carnival midway stretching north and south from the Blackpool Tower. Most of the town's retail stores sell Blackpool Rock, which consists of granite-hard candy in the shape of a salami, and T-shirts with rude sayings.

The real gem of Blackpool, and the principal reason the resort center has remained a mecca for DanceSport competitors and enthusiasts, is the Winter Garden Ballroom, site of the annual Blackpool Dance Festival.

With four thousand square feet of superb oak parquet floor, Blackpool's Winter Gardens remains the world's most elegant and celebrated competitive dance venue.

At the Blackpool Dance Festival, the audience is almost as informed and critical as the judging panel itself.

One step into this monument to Victorian-era elegance, and memories of Blackpool's fish-and-chip shops and carnival midway barkers vanish. The ballroom soars three levels above the four-thousand-square-foot oak parquet floor, its walls and ceiling festooned with Ionic pillars and carved gilt-edged cherubs. Spectators in the second and third levels are seated on plush red velvet upholstery; those on the coveted ground-floor level are more than content with folding metal chairs.

Twice annually, the Blackpool Dance Festival attracts literally thousands of the world's finest dancers, creating a concentration of performers unlike virtually any other global event. To American sport enthusiasts, only the Major League Baseball All-Star Game compares with such distillation of the finest talent in a specialized field. Throughout the rest of the world, perhaps only soccer's World Cup and the Cannes Film Festival are comparable.

The Blackpool Dance Festival determines the acknowledged world champions of Standard and Latin dances each year, yet few people beyond the dance fraternity are aware of its existence. Like much of ballroom dancing and DanceSport, Blackpool looks inward on a tradition that defies many of the changes taking place beyond the ballroom floor.

At Blackpool, the principal dance events are still performed to music played by a live fourteen-piece orchestra whose musicians wear shirts and ties while reading musical arrangements dating back fifty years or more. All seats during the festival are reserved, and prime locations in the front row at ballroom level are passed down, generation by generation, like heirlooms.

Blackpool is both a monument and a symbol of all that is prized about DanceSport and all that is threatened.

From its elegant setting and gracious formality to its unchallenged prestige, the Blackpool Festival distinguishes competitive dance from virtually every other competitive sport or artistic endeavor. Nothing else in dancing surpasses Blackpool in prestige and outright snobbishness, yet no other world-class competitive event is so egalitarian in many ways. Even the most honored competitors at Blackpool are still required to pay the same admission fee as first-time spectators.

Dressing and makeup rooms are as accessible to the public as to the dancers themselves. As a result, competitors who have just completed an electric and breathtaking performance on the ballroom floor a few moments earlier may be seen sprawled in various stages of undress, now merely exhausted mortals instead of spinning angels. Between events, the dancers await the judges' marks, practice intricate steps in back halls and dressing areas, bicker with each other over miscues, or sink crestfallen into their partner's arms when the standings reveal that they were not proficient enough, not energetic enough, simply not *good* enough, to advance further in the competition.

Dancers and spectators alike mingle in the stalls, in the back halls, and, during general dancing, on the spectacular ballroom floor itself. When the semifinal levels are reached, every eye is on that floor and on the dancers who perform with such astonishing grace and energy.

At Blackpool, everything is superlative. The setting is dramatic, the organization tight and efficient (as it should be with almost seventy-five years of experience), the gowns breathtaking, and most of the performances, at virtually any other competition venue, would be prize-winning.

Blackpool remains virtually a secret to almost everyone except true competitive dance aficionados. Media passes for photographers and writers are actively discouraged. To record the performance of thousands of entrants from sixty or more countries, only three official photographers are permitted; all others are relegated to spectator status, no matter who they are or what media they represent. Should *People, The Wall Street Journal,* and *The Times* of London all choose to cover the Blackpool Festival, opening their camera shutters and pages to the festival's drama and excitement, their photographers would be told to purchase a ticket, seat themselves where told, and shoot from wherever they could find an accessible location. There has been no accommodation to the needs of the working press in the past, and no suggestion that such a move will take place in the future.

Blackpool is exceptional in its elegant setting, rich tradition, and unexcelled competitors. But due to limited media coverage, it remains virtually unknown beyond the competitive dance world.

This is preposterous, of course. No popular press vehicle would tolerate such restrictions, which may explain why Blackpool and all that it represents is not only ignored but even ridiculed in some media quarters.

Nor is television more than grudgingly accommodated—although given the ability of television to severely disturb whatever event it ventures to cover, this may not be such a bad thing. Television cameras permitted at Blackpool are there solely to record selected events on videotape, but none is packaged and released to the networks.

The obstinacy of Blackpool organizers in refusing to compromise the festival's tradition and prestige in return for media coverage is admirable. But it may also be self-defeating.

For better or for worse, North American mass media is on the verge of discovering DanceSport and capturing its action, color, drama, sensuality, and glamour for presentation to a wide audience. If Blackpool and its organizers refuse to adapt to the needs and expectations of television, the producers will simply shrug and go elsewhere, to events and venues willing to accommodate and encourage their presence and coverage.

Inevitably, this single step will change DanceSport—or, at the very least, accelerate changes already in motion.

In the summer of 1997, the U.S. Nostalgia cable television channel announced its coverage of DanceSport on a regular basis. One of its first televised events was that year's Yankee Classic, a major competition held each year in Boston.

To a large extent, the program's producers converted the ballroom into a television studio. A special backdrop was constructed for show dancing, in which the partners could be captured "clean" against a lighted wall instead of among spectators, effectively eliminating a quarter of the floor perimeter normally available for audience seating.

Either in response to requests by the television producers or as coincidental programming, Yankee Classic promoters added new features especially suited to prepackaged programming. Most notable among these was a "Clash of the Continents" event in which a team composed of U.S. dancers competed,

couple against couple, with a team of European dancers through Standard and Latin steps.

This is a profound change from traditional ballroom competitions. Floorcraft means nothing when only two couples perform. Moreover, grace and elegance are deemed secondary to glitz and glamour.

The latter becomes a major factor when television coverage favors American Smooth and American Rhythm over International Standard and International Latin dances. American steps and costumes are tailor-made for mass-market television.

This may be the future of DanceSport: American-style open dance positions, dramatic lighting effects and, hovering nearby, the ubiquitous TV camera and crew.

Competitive dance offers everything that commercial television adores: color, motion, drama, and passion.

Nuances and subtleties of International dancing lose their impact when filtered through a television. When performing American Smooth steps, couples break from the closed position, often improvising their figures and literally revealing themselves to camera and audience. Women spin and twirl, raising the hems of their skirts in a manner that scandalizes traditional Standard dancers, but tantalizes mass television audiences.

If the world of competitive dancing eventually adopts the American style as orthodox in response to the influence of television, must this automatically be considered a bad thing? Probably not. But the by-product of change is frequently loss, and something will inevitably be lost if the deep and admirable traditions of the Blackpool Festival—as maddening as they may be to the media—are discarded in favor of thigh-high spinning skirts and jive steps among fox-trots.

That's the risk Blackpool faces—a risk leading to eventual backwater status and ultimately to that of a minor curiosity, a throwback to a time and tradition forever lost.

BLACKPOOL REPRESENTS THE MOST dramatic, but not the sole, potential loss of glamour and sophistication in competitive dancing. As the sport moves toward major sponsorship, larger cash awards, and wider exposure via network television, some aspects are already changing. In pursuit of success and acclaim, many young dancers are eager to bypass fundamentals in search of steps and figures designed exclusively to attract the attention of judges and the approval of spectators.

Naturally, this is decried in some quarters and applauded in others. Technical excellence, in athletics or in art, should not call attention to itself. Precise shoulder posture in a man as he leads his partner through a quick-step fails to catch the unpracticed eye as much as a body spin performed by a couple dancing the jive, for example.

To retain a respect for basic technique, many in the dancing world are depending upon quality training programs at the university and college level. In the United States, competitive varsity dancing thrives, with ballroom competitions held at universities from Harvard to UCLA. Some schools, such as Brigham Young University, offer full-credit courses on dancing.

The United Kingdom boasts a growing legion of competitive varsity dancers as well as opportunities such as the Supadance League, a series of competitions sponsored by a major vendor of dance-related shoes and accessories.

Each competitive opportunity may function according to its own standards and regulations, and all contribute in a small way toward expanding the excellence and exposure of dance.

But on the cusp of the twenty-first century, the key concern among most dance advocates is rooted in the Olympic Question.

THE INTERNATIONAL OLYMPIC COMMITTEE granted full recognition to Ballroom Dancing/DanceSport as an Olympic event in late 1997. This does not guarantee it a place on the Olympic program, which could take a decade or more to achieve.

The move toward full Olympic participation has generated a vibrant dialogue among the dancing community. Arguments on both sides of the question are regularly tossed back and forth over dinners, on the Internet, and almost anywhere a group of dancers decide to raise the topic.

Will full Olympic status finally propel DanceSport into the spotlight it deserves as a pastime equally demanding on both athletic and artistic talents? Or will it mark the beginning of the end, the descent of dancing into a morass of self-seeking individuals who reject tradition and finesse in sole pursuit of momentary fame and fortune?

Advocates of Olympic participation make a strong case. They argue, for example, that dancing's roots spring from a wide variety of cultures—wider than ice hockey or equestrian events, to name just two. They also draw attention to dancing's superb role model of compromise, cooperation, and mutual respect between male and female partners.

Others point to ice dancing, long a recognized sport in the Winter Olympics, as a strong precedent for including ballroom dancing. In fact, dancing requires a mastery of exclusive skills, such as floorcraft, which skating lacks.

Most of those who support full Olympic participation are enthused about the benefits of wider recognition, especially in North America where the popularity of dancing, while growing impressively, is restricted primarily to sophisticated urban areas.

Opponents of the idea express concern about topics such as subjective marking. Like figure skating, DanceSport would rely not upon stopwatches or scored goals but on the opinions of judges answerable to neither performers nor audience. This can lead to favoritism, especially for competitors from the judges' own countries, a problem that continues to plague skating. But skating addresses the subject, with varying degrees of efficiency, by measures such as discarding both the highest and lowest scores before calculating the result, or stipulating mandatory deductions for specific errors. Surely the same method could be applied to dancing.

As for the question of subjective scoring, experienced judges can quickly determine the top three rankings in almost every DanceSport competition. Perhaps the entire discussion is academic. How concerned should anyone be about the fairness of subjective assessments when objective rankings in track and field events often differ by only one one-hundredth of a second—hardly a measure of clear supremacy?

Other objections are raised over dancing rules (Who makes them? The International DanceSport Federation or the IOC?); the question of "amateur" status (a joke after the appearance of NBA veterans, each a multimillionaire, on the U.S. Olympic basketball "Dream Team"); and the public's perception and acceptance of dancing as a true sport. As noted earlier, sporting events automatically imply visible exertion, obvious skill, and often a clear risk of serious injury. Part of the reason Olympic-level ski jumping is so popular as a spectator sport is because few people would dare attempt such a feat. But in our hearts we all believe we can step onto a hardwood floor and dance!

And what of failure? When a favored skater prepares to execute a triple toe loop, our hearts are in our mouths because everyone will know whether she successfully completes it or not. Will the same drama flow from a perfectly executed double lock step performed during a waltz?

The discussion continues. The sporting fraternity and much of the popular press tend to ridicule the concept of Olympic-level dancing, and dancers themselves remain divided in their opinions.

DanceSport endures as the most exciting undiscovered form of active competition in the world, truly international in scope, accessible to most, and distinct in its separation of amateur and professional status.

How long can it stay that way?

CHAPTER NINE

Next Steps, First Steps

AS UNLIKELY AS IT MAY APPEAR AT first glance, the line between everyone's first awkward steps onto a dance floor and the sublime grace of the Final Six at Blackpool is straight and unbroken.

Dancing well, even for strictly social occasions, is often its own reward and worth an investment in lessons from a good teacher.

This doesn't suggest that anyone can become a Marcus or Karen Hilton, jetting off with sequined gowns and pressed tail suit to global competitions, no matter how much they practice or how intensely they toil. True champions in DanceSport possess a unique blend of physical qualities and mental abilities that set them apart from others. Just as in most other endeavors, inherited genes help distinguish those who succeed from those who merely strive. Perhaps the most common element among successful competitive dancers is the age at which they first encounter the sport. Most championship dancers launch their long careers well before puberty, and they either permit or foster an abiding relationship with dance; in fact, most agree that dancing does not merely dominate their life, it *becomes* their life.

But the joy earned by those who participate merely for the love and challenge of it, rather than for elevated glory, can be similar even if the rewards are less. Like golf, tennis, bridge, and chess, dancing offers rewards more deeply rooted in social activity than in the acquisition of trophies and acclaim. It also provides the extra benefits of exercise and relaxation, and the unique satisfaction of mastering a new skill, often in middle age. In fact, competitive dancing is one of the few sports in which competitors needn't feel their best years are behind them after reaching thirty years of age—or even forty.

Those who dance with true passion, even on a strictly social level, rave about other rewards. The ability to dance well improves self-confidence, for example. At weddings, parties, clubs, or wherever dancing plays a role in celebration and ritual, good dancers tend to radiate assurance and energy. Meanwhile, untrained dancers shuffle around the floor, their expressions revealing that they would prefer to be somewhere else, and their foot movements awkwardly trying to take them there.

Dancing is also an emotional outlet and a creative expression, and the enjoyment of both is in direct proportion to the dancer's skill and training.

Finally, those in pursuit of serious relationships soon discover their dancing skills can be more effective than almost any other talent they may acquire. This is especially true of men, who tend to underestimate the attraction that a smooth and confident dancer generates for most women. A man of almost any age who can fox-trot with grace and mambo with alacrity will soon find himself enjoying the luxury of choosing from among a wide range of partners, whether it's at a local singles gathering or on a Caribbean cruise.

While dancing may be a skill that is never fully mastered, the basic steps can be learned in only a few preliminary lessons and with a reasonable amount of daily practice. Neither men nor women require a partner to practice their steps and posture. Suitable music and an empty room (it takes more confidence than most beginners can muster to step and turn across the floor with an imaginary partner in their arms while an audience of nondancers watches) will suffice.

So why don't more people take dancing lessons? The

problem and the solution both reside in the same place: dancing schools and studios.

FRANCHISED AND INDEPENDENT DANCE studios operate as profit-making businesses, which should not come as a surprise. Unfortunately, the excesses of one small group can often overshadow the achievements of the others. Some dance studios have become infamous for being far more effective at separating customers from their money than at teaching them effective dance skills. In the eyes of a small group of studio operators and

The joy of dancing need not—and should not—be restricted to competitive events. Its rewards include performing with skill and grace at weddings and parties, in the company of friends.

their instructors, everyone who enters the studio is automatically a gifted dancer whose talent deserves a long-term contract of lessons, whose destiny is achieving championship status, and whose bank account is ripe for the picking.

Most nondancers assume their risk ends here. But a substantial number of people who approach dance studios are vulnerable to various entreaties. Chief concerns regarding the aggressive practices of some dance studios arise from the amount of sales pressure exerted versus the student's ability to pay. But there is also the question of the quality of instruction received.

Instructors at most franchised dance studios are selected as much for their selling skills as for their dancing ability. Selling skills are important to the franchise operator; the ability to communicate proper dancing skills, especially to raw beginners, is important to the student.

The typical first lesson at dance studios is to teach an individual or couple a basic box step. Just as it sounds, the man leads his partner one step forward, one step right, one step back and one step left, bringing them back to their original starting position. The entire motion can probably be taught to the average cocker spaniel, given enough time and sufficient rewards. Beginning students who achieve this fundamental figure are assured that they have conquered the first stage of ballroom dancing. Variations on the box step are adapted for the waltz and rumba, and once the rumba is learned, the student is told, most other Latin steps spin off from the same basic step.

All this is true, to some extent. But to the raw beginner, it should be seen for what it is: An hors d'oeuvre, tiny and tasty but not very nourishing. Competent dancing requires more than moving one's body within an imaginary squared circle, and improving one's dancing prowess demands pointed criticism more than unblemished enthusiasm.

So here, garnered from various dancers and visits to dance studios, both franchised and independent, are a few guidelines designed not to prevent you from learning to dance but to encourage you to do so with confidence:

Competitive Pro-Am events may pair very young children with older teachers and mentors.

A franchised dance studio may or may not represent a beginner's best choice. The critical element remains the ability and dedication of the teacher.

- Talk to any friends or associates who have taken dancing lessons. Ask what they learned—both about dancing and about dance studios—and do not permit any negative aspects of their experience to keep you from launching your own plan of lessons.

- Visit at least three dance studios in your area, if available. Trust your instincts, read the literature they provide, and agree to nothing at this point.

- Assume an armor of sales resistance. On your first visit to a dance studio, you may be asked for your name and telephone number and encouraged to take a first lesson "free" on the spot. Neither is necessarily an indication of the dance studio's ability to teach, but expect follow-up calls and sales pressure.

- Many franchised studios offer introductory specials such as "Five hours of instruction for just $15!" If other aspects of the studio appeal to you, this may be an ideal way to test the waters regarding their teaching philosophy and the quality of their instructors. Most also include an evening or two of social dancing, where you will have the opportunity to assess the abilities of other students and talk to them about their learning experiences.

- Remember that many studios, especially franchises, function as social clubs as much as dance studios. If socializing represents a driving force behind your urge to dance, this is not a problem. But there is no free dance, so to speak. The more the club concentrates on its efforts in organizing social functions, the less energy will remain for effective teaching.

- Perhaps one of the most productive steps is to visit a local dance competition in which students from several studios participate. Watch the dancers who represent the skill and style that appeal to you. Most competitions provide a printed program listing the contestants' names and the dance studios they represent. Talk to dancers and ask for their impressions and recommen-

dations for a dance studio. Dancers tend to be friendly and eager to assist new dancers. Contact a recommended studio, explain why you have selected them, and ask for a preliminary sample lesson.

WHATEVER DECISION YOU MAKE regarding a dance studio, expect to encounter a number of guidelines and challenges on your way to whatever level of dancing skill you aspire to. Here are the most common, as gleaned from a range of qualified and respected dancers and instructors:

There is no final destination. Learning to dance is a lifetime process, which represents part of its fascination. There will always be a new dance to learn, a new figure to experiment with, and a new dancing style to explore.

Do not try to rush the process. No one learning to play the piano expects to perform a Beethoven concerto within a few months of their first lesson. So don't try to rush your development. Learn each new figure thoroughly before moving on to the next, more complicated step. There is much to learn, and most consists of fundamentals; without mastering them, your ability to learn complex steps will be limited.

It takes a good teacher and a good partner. Ballroom dancing is not a solo endeavor. Your partner needn't match you perfectly in ability (although this is obviously a benefit), but he or she should be willing to practice often—which leads to the next point.

Remember the 5-to-1 ratio. It varies from teacher to teacher, but most agree that students should practice five hours for every one hour of instruction they receive. Thus, a one-hour weekly dance lesson should be followed by five hours of practice before the next lesson. This ratio also guides the amount of instruction received; no one except dedicated professionals could be expected to practice fifty hours per week to accommodate ten hours of instruction.

Understand the value of group lessons. Individual dancing lessons are more comfortable because only your teacher and your partner are aware of any learning problems. But group lessons in which you dance with different partners provide a broader opportunity to learn and test new skills. Ideally, you should seek both private and group sessions.

A woman must learn to follow; a man must learn to lead. Contrary to opinion in some quarters, this does not convey a sense of second-class status for the woman. It places a good deal of responsibility on the man, however, to choose steps and figures he is confident of performing, especially when dancing with someone other than his regular partner.

Be patient with yourself. Everyone grows frustrated at their inability to learn certain complex figures as quickly as they would like. The solution to frustration is to remind yourself that your purpose in learning to dance is to have fun. Put yourself in that frame of mind and you may discover a new reservoir of patience.

WHILE EVERY DANCE INSTRUCTOR takes pride in his or her special approach to teaching, some basics are so universal that they can be applied to everyone. Understanding these basics and practicing them will improve your sense of appreciation and comfort on the dance floor. They include:

Dancers move in a counterclockwise path around the dance floor. Accomplished dancers prefer the perimeter, which provides more room and opportunity to move at speed. Beginners should remain near the middle of the floor, where they are less likely to create an obstacle to others.

Dancing is a gracious, noncombative pastime. If you happen to collide with another dancer, always apologize. Aggressive dancers offer no redeeming qualities to anyone on or off the floor.

Like any skill, dancing requires practice—perhaps five hours for every hour of lessons.

Professional DanceSport competitors are often generous with their time spent among amateurs. Here, Corky and Shirley Ballas, famed Latin competitors, give an impromptu lesson to beginners at the Yankee Classic in Boston.

A suggestion for women: When your partner is leading you across the floor and you see an oncoming couple about to collide with you, use the agreed-upon "panic" signal. Simply tap your partner on the shoulder, alerting him to the danger and providing him with the opportunity to change direction.

Listen for the beat. Catchy melodies and clever lyrics play an important part in the enjoyment of music, but they're of secondary interest to dancers. Concentrate on the beat provided by the bass and drums. Learn to count the rhythm in each bar. For all dances except waltzes, count ONE-two-three-four, ONE-two-three-four. The ONE represents the first beat of the bar, and you can soon learn to hear it. In a waltz, listen for ONE-two-three, ONE-two-three. Latin steps employ more complicated rhythms, but the beat is also more easily heard and defined.

Remember to move sideways and backward as well as forward. (This tends to be a bigger challenge for men than for women.) Beginners should avoid taking any side steps that are wider than their own shoulders.

Try keeping your head directly above the foot carrying your weight. This may seem either overly complicated or insultingly simple, but it's the key to keeping your balance while you dance.

Carry your weight on the ball of your foot. Except for flamenco and paso doble, your toes are meant for dancing, not your heels.

Originate all leg motion from the hip. This permits the leg to swing more freely and smoothly.

Measure your steps to the tempo of the music. Fast songs demand shorter steps; slow songs demand longer steps.

DANCE CDS AND AUDIOTAPES, as well as dance videos, are popular items sold by many dance studios and at most dance competitions. Both can play a role in helping you learn to dance and set goals for yourself.

CDs and audiotapes are especially helpful in providing the ideal tempo and mood for each dance to be learned and practiced. Chosen not for background listening but for specific dance figures, the music usually features simplified arrangements of familiar tunes. Investing in one or two of the most popular versions is an excellent way to make your practice sessions more fruitful.

Dance videos are also helpful, but in a different context. Most feature exceptionally gifted and talented performers, such as Corky and Shirley Ballas, performing in competition and demonstrating step-by-step instructions.

The appeal of the videos is easy to understand. Watching two masters such as Corky and Shirley (who, at last count, were marketing over twenty-five different videos) is fascinating and enjoyable. They can also be inspiring and educational. The danger lies in assuming you can match their level of prowess in just a few weeks. Not so, as even they would agree. Simple steps can indeed be learned quickly from a video, depending on your skills and dedication. But the complex patterns of a samba, paso doble, or quick-step, as executed by Corky and Shirley, are the result of years of pain, practice, and participation. Finally, as excellent as many instruction videos may be, nothing can replace the experience of dancing with a wide range of partners under the watchful eye of a competent instructor.

CHAPTER TEN

One More Time Across the Floor

IF CHAOS BREEDS LIFE, BALLROOM dancing is about to explode in a fury of propagation.

Within the closed culture of DanceSport, discussions regarding its future churn on with as much fury and energy as a ten-minute samba.

The Olympic question may be the most divisive, but only because the topic is clear-cut and specific. Should DanceSport seek full Olympic participation or not? Even the Olympic advocates agree that such an event will change competitive dancing in more ways than anyone can predict. Who will agree on a global syllabus and scoring system? How will "amateur" be defined? Will one culture's disapproval of costumes restrict the freedom currently enjoyed by dancers, especially Latin performers?

Attached to the same topic is the impact of mass-market television coverage, an anticipated by-product of Olympic recognition. How far must DanceSport go in accommodating the demands and expectations of network TV, with its multiple camera placement and studio-pure lighting? Will television insist that

The athleticism of dancers is ultimately unquestioned. But does it qualify as "sport," especially among those who dispute its entry into Olympic competition?

only one couple at a time perform, à la ice skating? If so, what happens to the quality of floorcraft, and the magnificent imagery of several dozen couples sweeping across the dance floor, enchanting the audience with the spectacle even as they confound the judges in determining their selection?

Anyone who scans dance publications, surfs dance sites on the Internet, or even eavesdrops on conversations at international dance competitions will grow either immensely impressed or thoroughly confused with the thoughts and ideas being exchanged. Impressed because such a wide range of opinion, often spiced with deep emotion, suggests a vibrant, dedicated, and deeply committed culture; confused because so much of the discussion appears to deal with concerns that hardly seem to deserve the effort and energy.

Consider the very name of this elegant activity. Is it "Ballroom Dancing" or is it "DanceSport"? One strong contingent—anchored, surprisingly, in Britain—lobbies against the very word *ballroom* in any connection. The discussion is no academic exercise. It represents a deeply felt aversion to a word that not only limits the public perception of contemporary social/competitive dancing, but describes a venue that is becoming as rare as the panda.

Few nondancers can name or locate a ballroom in their own hometown, if one even exists. Ballrooms are massive, extravagant palaces dedicated to a bygone society, and while we should preserve the specimens still remaining, we should lower our expectations that we will ever see their like again.

This anomaly explains some of the fury felt by those who campaign against the term. Listen to one advocate for banishing the word, as recorded in a major U.K. dance publication:

> For years I've campaigned for ["ballroom's"] eradication, its banishment, its complete and utter termination, but it still clings like pitch to a blanket. It's an incubus, a dead hand holding us helplessly and hopelessly to an old-fashioned out-moded image, tethered terminally to the tailcoat of a bygone era.

Will some of DanceSport's overt sexuality survive recognition from Olympic management, a group famous for its reactionary and disapproving attitude toward rebelliousness of any kind? Time will tell.

How laughably ironic it is, therefore . . . to discuss the "future" of ballroom dancing when ballroom, per se, has no future. It's as dead as the dinosaurs. The trouble is that there are still too many among us who won't let go of its memory. Their minds are perfumed by the past, insulated from progress by a misty haze of mythic, romantic illusion.[1]

Seldom has such an emotional objection regarding a sporting activity been phrased in such eloquent prose. Unfortunately, few if any of the suggested replacements for "Ballroom Dancing" appear to satisfy a substantial number of its advocates.

"DanceSport" helps describe activities pursued by highly charged competitive dancers, but even this term is subject to derisive comments from within the dance culture. And the sarcasm drips heavily in some of these discussions. "Dancing a sport?" one dancer sneered in defense of maintaining the word *ballroom*. "A surgeon performing a 16-hour life-saving operation exerts more stamina than any Olympic athlete, but doesn't regard by-pass surgery as a sport!"[2]

And the music plays on . . .

THOSE WHO STAND APART from the nomenclature debate find other itches to scratch.

The question of judging criteria is a popular one, but so it may be with any decision assessed according to subjective guidelines, from baseball to the Academy Awards.

For example, how influenced are judges by a dancer's physique? While dancing is unquestionably an activity demanding good physical condition, human beings range widely in appearance. A few dancers manage to achieve a remarkable level of dancing ability while carrying obvious excess weight. Do their unshed pounds deprive them of recognition for their pure dancing ability? Without question, in most cases. We want to see lithe, perfectly sculpted bodies on the floor, representing the epitome of elegance (in the case of Standard or American

Personal expression remains both the incentive and the hallmark of successful dancers.

Smooth dances) or lean and raw sensuality (for Latin or American Rhythm performances).

How much impact is made by the cut and color of the dancers' costumes, the shade and style of their hair, the depth of their tan, the height of their hemline?

AS COMPETITIVE DANCING CONTINUES to expand across national boundaries, a perception has grown regarding the strengths and weaknesses of some nationalities in various dance steps. The question of apparent ethnic or nationalistic talents for some dance figures isn't a matter of stereotyping, although that danger admittedly exists. It's a recognition that dance reflects many cultural aspects which, when interpreted by two skilled partners, influence and often heighten their ability to express the core of the dance.

No evidence exists to suggest that dance judges make their selections based on ethnic origin alone, nor would it be tolerated by any credible dance organization. (Nationalistic favoritism, as demonstrated too often in figure skating at the Worlds and Olympics, is another matter. Recognition of DanceSport as a full Olympic event will undoubtedly address this danger by eliminating the highest and lowest mark prior to calculating final scores.) Competitive dancing may well be the most gracious and fair-minded of all international events, free of the more extreme and vicious aspects that taint similar sporting activities from time to time.

But how long can it remain that way?

Already, concern has been expressed about the heightened intensity of some competitive events. When competitive instincts grow stronger, respect for decorum begins to fade. Is dancing's virtually unblemished record a reflection of the sport's courtly roots and the male/female relationship? Or is it merely a result of insignificant monetary rewards and limited exposure in the mass media?

The latter question underlines much of the concern expressed in some quarters regarding Olympic representation and the highly charged competitive atmosphere of some North American dance events.

DanceSport cuts across ethnic and cultural lines like virtually no other competitive activity. Scandinavians excel at Latin steps that originated in the Caribbean, Japanese are superb at performing British court dances, and stoic Germans are famous for their uninhibited rock 'n' roll.

Can DanceSport gain wide respect and still retain its innocence?

THE DANCING COMMUNITY ALSO FACES a number of other developments likely to challenge its fundamental beliefs and cultural foundations. Many of these are threatened by the two-edged sword of wider recognition and richer rewards.

Much of dancing's appeal over centuries of development has been the avenue of self-expression it provides for individuals and couples. Music frames the action and the dancers perform within that frame, employing their bodies to express emotions and desires in a manner beyond mere words. Each couple, moving according to a common rhythm and following the same dance figures, generates a unique language between themselves, performing according to their own emotional expression and response.

Intense competition threatens to change all that.

When dancing or any creative activity is performed primarily for the participant's satisfaction, personal expression becomes logically paramount. What, after all, is to be gained by duplicating someone else's style when you are free to develop and express your own?

Prospects of fame and fortune may change matters significantly. Instead of personal expression, dancers may follow public tastes and judging preferences. If high jumps and dizzying spins win recognition and rewards, these are the figures to be performed, and to hell with personal expression. Will broader coverage, richer purses, and more flamboyant productions expand or limit dancing styles? Many expect these trends to inhibit new ideas, as dancers focus only on the figures most likely to achieve championship status.

Not all of this is quite as cut and dried as it sounds. All gifted dancers are artists, and all artists remain sensitive to the trends and values of their times. Included among those values, especially within Western society, is the concept that all measurable achievements exist to be challenged and exceeded.

In some activities, such as track and field, this motivation can

Sometimes the dream comes true: an uncrowded floor, a partner like a feather in your arms, and music heard only by the two of you.

occur without seriously affecting the sport's foundations—assuming, of course, that the activity avoids the use of unlawful aids such as drugs and steroids. In others—once again, figure skating springs to mind—the nature of the sport is irrevocably altered by wider media exposure and excessive financial awards. When that happens, something is lost and mourned.

A decade ago, a successfully executed triple lutz represented an insurmountable challenge, like the four-minute-mile barrier of half a century ago. Today, quad jumps are considered the hallmark of a championship performance. Are we to see attempts at quintuple jumps within a short period of time? If so, to what purpose, other than breaking yet another numerical barrier?

In dance terms, a preoccupation with quantitative standards—how much, how many, how high—manifests itself in greater speed across the floor, loftier jumps, faster transfers of weight, quicker changes of direction, more complex footwork, and so on. Add to this the increasingly elaborate performances staged primarily for network television exposure—frequent spins by women dancers, raising their skirts above waist level—and the more demure aspect of ballroom dancing may be swept aside in a frenzy of more dazzle, more provocation, more glitz.

Or does it matter?

The previous century ended with disapproval of the waltz among the more genteel sectors of society. Yet dancing endured and developed, and those aspects valued as demure and traditional at the beginning of the twenty-first century would have been considered decadent in the salons of Victoria and Albert.

From our point of view, the danger of excessiveness may in reality represent a harbinger of a new dancing universe, one that elevates dancing toward ever higher and more excessive standards of performance and expression. The words that swirl between advocates on both sides of the debate—those wishing to preserve tradition and glamour, and those advocating recognition and reward—are only words, after all. And words have often proved inadequate amid the passions that fuel the need to dance.

So let the music begin.

Perhaps the adult world is finally ready for a return to closed-position social dancing, where a couple moves across the floor in response to the rhythm of the music and the delight of their own relationship.

Let the gentlemen approach the ladies, bowing and extending their hand before leading their partners to the floor. Let their eyes meet and their bodies sway, let their feet perform figures and steps both familiar and new, let their shoulders stay fixed in the regal strains of a waltz or flex and flutter in the mad rhythm of a samba. Let them twist and bump and hustle and hip-hop if they must (and they will), and let them all return to the same romantic meanings, when they seek to express private thoughts in a public setting, lost in motions beyond words and feelings beyond logic.

Let them dance.

Notes

CHAPTER THREE
1. T. A. Faulkner, *From the Ball-Room to Hell* (Chicago: The Church Press, 1894), 45.
2. Irene Castle, *Castles in the Air* (New York: Da Capo Press, Inc., 1980), 85.
3. Barbara Garvey, "Return of the Tango," *The Smithsonian Magazine*, September 1993, 34.

CHAPTER FOUR
1. It has been observed that referring to the primarily Anglo-Saxon origins of the waltz, fox-trot, and quick-step as "Standard" dances implies that the Latin dances are somehow deviant in nature. This is the kind of observation made only by fervent sociologists and academics. Dancers never question the meaning and hold both schools in high regard.

CHAPTER FIVE
1. Ginger Rogers, *Ginger: My Story* (HarperCollins, 1991), 114.

CHAPTER SEVEN
1. *The Times* (London), January 25, 1997.
2. Elizabeth Cullip, "Amateur International Standard at the 1996 Ohio Star Ball," *Dance Beat*, January 1997, 5.

CHAPTER TEN
1. Victor Tomlinson, as reported in "Dance Sport vs. Ballroom," *Dance Beat*, November 1996, 3.
2. Ibid.

Major Annual North American DanceSport Events

NOTE: The following is a representative list only of major annual events in the U.S. and Canada. For a more detailed schedule of amateur and professional dance events, including major regional competitions, consult a DanceSport publication or local dance studio.

February	Snowball Classic	Vancouver, BC
March	Manhattan Amateur Classic	New York, NY
April	Open DanceSport Competition	San Francisco, CA
	South West Regional Dance Championship	San Diego, CA
May	Emerald Ball	Los Angeles, CA
	U.S. Ten-Dance Professional Championships	Los Angeles, CA
	Canadian Open Dance Championships	Toronto, ON
	Minnesota Open Ballroom Dance Competition	St. Paul, MN
June	Yankee Classic	Boston, MA
August	National DanceSport Championships	Indianapolis, IN
September	U.S. Open Championships	Miami, FL
November	Harvest Moon Ball	Chicago, IL
	Ohio Star Ball	Columbus, OH
December	Annual Yuletide Ball Championships	Washington, DC

Major Annual International DanceSport Events

NOTE: This is a partial listing only.

AUSTRALIA

August	Australian Open	Brisbane

EUROPE

February	Denmark IDSF* Open Standard and Latin Championships	Copenhagen
	European Union Standard Dance Championships	Arnhem, Netherlands
March	Italian IDSF* Open Standard and Latin Championships	Rimini
	Russian IDSF* Open Standard and Latin Championships	St. Petersburg
April	French IDSF* Open Standard and Latin Championships	Paris
May	IDSF* World Ten-Dance Championship	Copenhagen
October	IDSF* International Open Latin	Liege, Belgium
	Swiss IDSF* Open Standard and Latin Championships	Zurich
November	IDSF* World Senior Standard Championships	
December	Ukrainian IDSF* International Open Standard and Latin Championships	Kiev

HONG KONG

March	Super International Ballroom Dance Championships–Open	

JAPAN

February/March	Super Japan Cup (Makuhari Messe)	Chiba
June	Japan International Ballroom Dance Championships	Tokyo
October	Standard Dance Championships	Toyko

SINGAPORE

August	Lion City International DanceSport Championships	

U.K.

May	Blackpool Dance Festival–Open	Blackpool
November	British National Dance Championships	Blackpool

*International DanceSport Federation

The publisher acknowledges the following people and organizations and thanks them for their participation in this book.

Participating dance studios

Helena Granger-Sandov & Chris "Bob" Sandov of *The Academy of International Dance*

Sonia Kyriacou of *San Tropez*

Vladimir Leon Suanez of *Step-in-Two Dance Studio*

Helen Ross of *The Continental Dance Club*

José "Néné" Noesi, Marselo Juares & Kim Valequitte of *Tropicalissimo Productions*

Violetta Majewski of *Violetta's Dance Place*

Participating coordinators

Paul Suke of Visual Stream

Dia Tsitsouras of Smog Hair Salon

Participating dancers

Moris Alvarenga

Karina Sophia Andre

Alison Barnard

Cesar Cervantes

Arthur and Shirley Chan

Melanie Chappee

André Gillezeau

Patricia Goh

Chinny Hoen

Marselo Juares

Sonia Kyriacou

Catherine Ladriere

Catarina Lalonde

Phil Lee

Hugo Matos

Kelly McKaye

José "Néné" Noesi

Thomas Philpott

Dimitra Rizis

Helena Granger-Sandov and Chris "Bob" Sandov

James Sebe

Rita Shaw

Vladimir Leon Suanez

Robert Tang and Beverley Cayton-Tang

Richard Thibeault

Anna Tomsic

Maude Vachon

Robin Vaile

Ron and Barbara Wilson